THE VILLAINS WHO SNAPPED MY SPINE

MY SPINE

A MEMOIR

A. H. NAZZARENO

For my wife

"Flyleaf": a blank page at the beginning or end of a book

CONTENTS

INTRODUCTION

THE YEAR 2021 WAS TERRIBLE, and I'll miss it as much as acute juvenile acne or a knee-aching, hamstring-snapping rally car clutch. While everyone else welcomed the spring with unmasked faces, I was experiencing a health crisis. Bleakness peaked by the end of June as I watched my wife, Michelle, go back to work, and the reality of day-to-day monotony consumed my thoughts. I looked as damaged as the bruised fruit of a pear tree after a hailstorm, lumbering through the house with a reassembled core, considering my options, and mulling over our rotten finances. Halfway into July, I was slogging through a stack of insurance statements and consumed by a blitz of medical appointments, coming to terms with the undeniable evidence of a villain-riddled existence.

Like many hapless souls consigned to deal with a riveting diagnosis, my shock at learning that I was a victim of myxopapillary ependymoma soon shifted to envy as I witnessed the droves of more fortunate individuals who complained about social distancing and canceled concerts. The extrinsic, selfish drama of taking things for granted now seemed magnified, only advancing my malaise. The Earth kept spinning, as it always has, oblivious and unaware that my fragile life was under siege.

While most people stressed about double masking and booster shots, the villains were busy battering down our home's drafty 19th-century pine door, and I was convinced that a tragic, untimely death was my only guarantee.

Although the year was disastrous, its one redeeming quality was that it provided a life-altering reality check. The bitter reconciliation reminded Michelle and I that life is too short to second-guess, procrastinate, or play things safe. Suddenly, the desert was calling; a seductress once encountered that is never forgotten. I slowly shuffle-ran to the phone to answer. A change of scenery was exactly what we needed after enduring such a challenging year. We missed those Ponderosa pines, towering fir trees, scraggly mesquite in all their glory, and sunsets that seemed bigger than the entire state of Rhode Island.

It wasn't the desert, unsurprisingly. The smudged screen on my phone identified the contact I had entered at the end of a chaotic May as "Doctor in Boston." My mood immediately deteriorated whenever I took these calls, yet I swiped to answer anyway.

"Hello?"

"Hello, this is the Doctor in Boston who saved your life."

"Yes."

"OK, great. What times are good for you for your next MRI?"

I paused and considered hanging up; flight always seemed better than putting up a fight, now more than ever. I wanted to grab my luggage, throw it all in the car, and start driving west. Discard the rearview mirror, fill all six cupholders with iced coffee, and just keep going until I reached the Prescott National Forest, the Enchanted Forest, or the arid wasteland mislabeled as the Petrified Forest. *Any* fucking forest, really. Simply spend the rest of my life basking in sweet, selfish bliss, because ignorance is sometimes nicer than all-seeing-eye MRI wizardry. If possible, I wanted to opt out of the whole endeavor, discard it like a losing scratch ticket, burn my medical records, and wake up somewhere serene. Maybe toss a steak on one of those park charcoal grills and extract a crunchy baked potato from the embers, because that's as good as it gets. Take a never-ending, quaint stroll with Michelle where we first met, forgetting about reality forever.

That would be nice.

Sometimes reality is not always pleasant, good, or an enlightening experience. *It just is.* The contemptible year known as 2021 provided me with two notable realizations: steer clear of placidity and confront your villains before it's too late.

Attempting to reverse significant mood trauma by the time a scorching August arrived, I binged every stand-up comedy special next to a blasting air conditioner, sipping gallons of extra-dark-roasted coffee and eating a lot of desserts. Over the next few weeks and pounds—courtesy of Dr. Summeroff, "Doctor in Boston"—I wrote about my ordeal to break up the monotony of cursing about my problems to unresponsive plaster walls. I had recently painted the living room "sun cactus" green, and sometimes a discounted paint that someone else didn't want to pick up at the hardware store is a good-enough inspiration for a book's theme.

This memoir is the truth as I remember it to the best of my memory. Hopefully, this reality check is better than some eponymous, crowdfunded sob-story solicitation asking for money or "likes." I've never done that my entire life, and I don't see why I should start now simply because the proverbial bridge I was crossing collapsed, forcing me to experience an unexpected detour through hell.

HOSPITAL IN BOSTON

ADMISSION DAY

JUNE 2021

THE SONS *of bitches want to kill me, but they prefer to take their time, and God isn't letting them win without a fight. Maybe I can expose their villainous shape-shifting asses, or at least vent.*

I checked in for my surgery at the highly rated Boston hospital as one would a hotel, minus a room key and no sign of desirable accommodations such as cookies, a drink menu, or a swimming pool. Pretending to be in a better place might help some people in such dire conditions, but delusion was as ineffective as a placebo. I'll call the experience for what it was at the time: a nightmare. The waiting room was as somber as the DMV but with even less enthusiasm and slightly more urgency. Despite the circumstances, my blood pressure was low, although my legs were shaking. After I signed some papers about emergency contacts, they wanted me to have a blood test, and I reluctantly consented even though I hated blood more than the dentist's office.

The hugs were brisk—two seconds; after all, this wasn't a funeral. Clearing my lumpy throat was difficult while embracing a teary, red-eyed wife, mom, and brother. I performed my best

1

impression of a poker face because of an ego that wanted to appear as brave as Wild Bill Hickok holding aces and eights, undeterred by the anticipation of a cold steel gun barrel pointed at the back of my head. The only poker I ever played was on my phone, yet I now feared the culmination of bad luck, and an unexpected surgery would be as damning as the notorious "dead man's hand."

The morning of the surgery I tried to psyche myself up. It was one of the very few days in my adult life I skipped my morning coffee *on purpose*, and a predictable caffeine-withdrawal headache was aching behind my strung-out blue eyes. I craved that heavenly piping-hot hit of liquid java, but there were more pressing matters to deal with, and I remained obsessed with having to pee too much. At least that was one aspect of my life I could control as everything was spiraling around me. It was as if someone had handed me a useless parachute infested with moth larvae as a host of villains were hacksawing off my plane's wings over Death Valley in July. I strapped on a perforated bracelet because this place was legit and an appointment was required. Some people brought luggage, but I didn't out of habit —I always travel light. The nurse whisked me to another room reminiscent of a closet-size apartment I once lived in with Michelle. After stepping briefly onto the scale, the nurse read a weight, but my mind was reeling. I was too preoccupied to register kilograms and pounds.

Perhaps the scales will tilt in our favor again? No, that's about as likely as winning the lottery.

I remembered all the frustrated, muttering people in idling cars clutching lucky quarters, frantically scraping away lottery tickets on their steering wheels for the prospect of a better life. I encountered these desperate souls while delivering mail to convenience stores and gas stations every day. Their disbelief at losing *again* was as predictable as a utility bill or student loan statement showing up every month. Right now mediocrity sounded great compared to the dismal uncertainty I was experiencing.

Will this even fucking work? What would the diagnosis be when the lab results arrive in a week? The doctor had a guess, but nothing definitive. Those lab tests could be life-changing.

Fuck the lottery. You're lucky you don't have actual problems, and not being a millionaire isn't a real problem.

The nurse logged more data into the computer, and I remained silent, battling all the chaotic uncertainties clogging my brain waves.

They informed me fluid was building in my brain, which didn't help settle my nerves.

Maybe the man upstairs will grant one more favor on my behalf? I know I don't have nine lives like a cat, but I want this one to last for a long time. Maybe sink my teeth into another burger in the In-N-Out parking lot, dripping secret sauce and grease over a complimentary cardboard box with Michelle while admiring a desert sunset. That would be nice.

Time to change uniforms. Answer more medication questions. Sign legal papers. Tell them I'm white, married, and scared "shirtless" in my untied robe as I stared at the computer's screensaver cartoon depicting an alien spaceship abducting a cow. That image became seared into my mind, vivid and permanent like a hot branding iron hitting an unsuspecting flank. When offered the last opportunity, I considered ducking out to the bathroom and not returning. Ghosting the whole hospital adventure before it even began because the feeling of doom reverberated through my nerve-pinched core the second I arrived at the parking garage.

Maybe I could resurrect the "cursed Lincoln," run away to Arizona, and deliver cartel drugs like Clint Eastwood in a Hollywood movie? Pick up the wife somehow too; I can't leave her out of this plan. After all, she's my copilot, best friend, coconspirator, partner in crime, study buddy, roommate, and now spouse—as critical as oxygen above

12,500 feet, that one reliable current of normalcy running through my life.

That would be one hell of a way to go out.

THE NURSES and staff reminded me a few hundred times that my birthday was the next day, making me cringe and bite my tongue —I didn't give a damn about cake, candles, or ages. I wished the whole unfortunate situation was a bad dream or mirage, something reminiscent of a drug-induced fantasy straight out of *Fear and Loathing in Las Vegas*. But it was not. It was all real, and I could have really used some ether and a convertible Chevy.

My hand was trembling, clutching a cellphone I was half-ignoring. Michelle and my "Red Shark" (a 1990 Oxford White Lincoln Mark VII LSC coupe) were nowhere near, and my oasis called Arizona was over 2,000 miles away.

The second I walked past the doors prohibiting guests, it hit me. This was the real fucking deal, and I couldn't bluff my way out of this mess. The virtual punch in the face tested my nerves, even though I tried not to flinch. I was hell-bent on staring my fate in the eye like a man, or at least as coolly as the stone-cold gun-slinging version of myself I pictured, because growing up on John Wayne's impressive filmography will do that to you. We didn't have "the cable" for most of my youth—that was for the affluent families with more than one car in the driveway. So, yeah, no Nick at fucking Night for me; it was all static antenna and VHS compilations of Westerns featuring "real" men and women with adult problems that booze, tobacco, and a desert backdrop could all somehow mend.

The calm before the storm, which arrived right after Memorial Day, courtesy of an MRI, hinted at future terror. I suppose if the National Weather Service was running the radiology department at our local hospital, they would have issued a warning for "an earthquake disguised as a tropical depression." They'd probably recommend taking shelter and checking your will to verify your address is up-to-date. But addresses and beneficiaries were the last things I cared about as I scribbled all my login passwords on a sheet of paper for Michelle in case she needed them, which was how I imagined writing a last-second will would be like. The surprise forecast cast me into the evil eye of a furious and destructive hurricane, ready to capsize, waiting for the operation, wondering how long I had left to live. The experience was chilling, like being locked in a freezer and having a standoff with an angry Arizona bark scorpion, and I should warn you, I'm no adrenaline junkie or exotic-food enthusiast. I wanted to be optimistic, but I could feel the wind ripping right around the corner, ready to suck the air out of my chest. My heart was beating loudly, and I swear the only time I was ever this close to death was when I was teetering on the edge of the Grand Canyon and peering straight down, hypnotized by the beautiful abyss.

Staring into the abyss of the hospital curtain surrounding my bed, I remembered one thing I told Michelle when more MRIs revealed added complexity:

"I have a bad feeling. What if this goes wrong or nothing works after all this … what's the fucking point?"

I was holding it together pretty well until the exact moment when she handed me an early birthday card depicting a picturesque camper trailer scene with a romantic caption. The thoughtful gesture triggered a mild breakdown, which I had repressed for about two weeks. A torrent of fear and frustration had been eating away at my stoic facade, prompting the dire prediction.

Now I am really hoping my bad feeling is wrong.

In the nerve-wracking moments before I headed to the corral, where patients wait to be sliced and diced like cattle, I believe I appeared calm, even though my brow may have been flinching. There was definitely something more violent than a butterfly in my groaning stomach. I don't know what the exact time was as I handed over my phone and the drugs started flowing, but in my mind, it was "20 past 11," like Cash sang, and I didn't want to end up like Texas Red.

I was rolled into the sterile beaming-white operating room, and masked professionals greeted me. I prayed it would all turn out OK and that if it didn't, maybe the angels would intervene, or the aliens would abduct me before things went further south.

VILLAIN NUMBER 1: THE LINCOLN

MAY 2011

GUNNING through the sun-soaked Southwest in a vintage luxury coupe at 20 years young is one of those pivotal moments you never forget and, when looking back, wish could have lasted forever. The V8's burbled exhaust echoed along the highway underpasses with a consistent gratification, giving just the right growl when the overhauled transmission downshifted. Passing unsuspecting traffic was more entertaining than I could have expected two grand of savings to provide.

The soundtrack seemed so savory, flowing in rhythmic waves to the outside world, that it wasn't even worth trying to tune the broken radio or pull over to adjust the supposed power antenna mast. The electronics were never reliable, but that was never something I cared about. I sought *experience*, not the societal status people with salon hair and expensive phone cameras obsessed about on the internet, or what the idiot neighbor, who drove a Honda Civic, thought was cool. *I guess I still believe that: Live your damn life because it's yours and no one else's.*

Dodging the misplaced tumbleweed was a welcome task,

and chasing the endless green sea of cactus felt like a race with no finish line. The crimson and copper landscape was outlined by blackened-tan mountain ranges, dotted with dehydrated cows, and sometimes interrupted by casinos. We didn't have the money, fake IDs, or inclination to gamble with our lunch fund or our future, but a simple glance toward the scenery captured the spirit of the West, suggesting an infinite number of good days were on the horizon.

As the badass driver of the clear-coat-peeling white-yet-rust-free jalopy dream machine, I'm sure the spectacle of a newly licensed postadolescent with long hair, attitude, and a penchant for burnouts wasn't as satisfactory to everyone else. Except, perhaps, for the hot girlfriend I was following in her equally excellent and white five-speed Ranger. Although the engine was painfully underpowered, and it undoubtedly embarrassed me as we leaned forward in our seats—holding our breath as the little engine strained its way in low gear up any natural incline—the experience was worth it despite hazard flashers and street credibility ruining my mood.

Just kidding—my "white whale" was more impressive and rarer, even though, regrettably, neither vehicle had working air-conditioning. But it didn't matter. With these questionable choices, we had both evaded boredom, a fear that rivaled a dipping GPA, student loans, or the Great Recession job market in those much simpler days.

The street credibility was tipped in my favor, at the very least, because of cylinder count. The luxury coupe was also more comfortable, offering power-adjustable plush leather seats far superior to the pickup's spartan, sticky vinyl. Likewise, the white whale emitted a beautiful exhaust note that vibrated the cracked, weathered dash. The car was unmatched by anything less aggressive, although tinnitus was becoming a valid concern and mature decision-making remained as evasive as the swaying fuel gauge. The tone of the 302-cubic-inch motor sang to your soul somehow, but as her loyal "study partner" and road trip companion, I must defend my girlfriend's adult-driven choice of mundane, practical transportation. Since freshman year of college, Michelle was more intelligent, financially savvy, and helped me close the deal on the magnificent rolling white whale —*and damn, she drove a stick*, so that was cool enough in my book.

THE EPIC JOURNEY began in the state where we first met: Arizona. It would end somewhere on the East Coast, if we had the nerve to return to our respective families. Michelle's family was from Boston, and they sounded like it. Their daughter shared no discernable dialect, which was easier for my non–New England ears to comprehend but initially seemed suspicious. My mother-in-law didn't even know her daughter's blood type, and I suspected a cover-up. Michelle was either a secretly adopted orphan or an alien, but I didn't really care. If forged documents and lies produced such an honest and caring person, or if she was an undercover agent from another galaxy, it didn't matter— that takes grit and admirable determination. Besides, why would this good-natured olive-eyed brunette Boston babe go through the trouble to deceive me, anyway? I was just a poor, but clever, sarcastic kid from New Jersey, Exit 4, who loved her company and pretty much everything else about her, except for the cats.

Our long-standing shared tradition was to walk and talk through our problems together. We were both the firstborn of our families, which meant we were the least spoiled (subjective, I know, but as accurate as most news), so we had many problems. Occasionally, we studied with index cards or wrote term papers after checking in at the movie theater a few times a week to date. But we spent 90 percent of our spare time walking or aimlessly driving across the John Ford–inspired cinematography, escaping from new challenges and mentally recharging. There was no doubt we were equally taking part in this life adventure. We were as inseparable as a veteran rally car driver team or a smoker with a cigarette. Although it took us more than a decade to tie the marriage knot, we were in spirit, even at that inexperienced, restless age, and that seemed good enough for us.

Our squinty, unsuspecting faces were not smiling in our first photo together, but that was probably because it was taken with a speed camera. Sometimes, the Ranger was a disguised rocket, and a select few Arizona towns were desperate for revenue and salivating over a copy of 1984. So, from the beginning, Michelle and I were partners in crime running from villainous entities, and that feeling surpassed most accomplishments or what any other potential windfall could offer. I wanted it to last longer than the horror of having to pay for texts or the film roll of a disposable camera. Still, the first mug shot was worth every one of her mom's pennies when shown one day to an unsuspecting parent in Massachusetts.

"Who is the passenger?"

"A friend."

"Looks like a boy."

"Yeah."

"*Boyfriend?*"

"Poor signal, Mom, got to go do homework."

WHEN NOT BREAKING the law in Arizona, we hiked along dusty scrub-lined trails accessible from our college campus, hashing out our consummate adolescent angst while on the lookout for *National Geographic*–worthy wildlife inhabiting the acres of untouched desert. Sometimes we took a break from all the walking because our diet wasn't that ideal, and I remember pining for the day when we'd have a real kitchen instead of a tiny communal nook with a microfridge and a toaster pretending to be an oven. In those days, my inclination to pursue athleticism was lacking, and any actual physical conditioning—thanks to a future villainous postal route and a high-octane java habit—did not yet exist.

One such resting spot was a park bench suspiciously chained to the ground alongside a sandy path. It was staring down at a murky and sprawling marsh that an ancient dead tree once sucked moisture from but was now a big hotel for a flock of bitchy birds we guessed were cormorants. As we sat sharing an Al Capone, ruminating on current topics, and rehashing old ones, occasionally the fowl got worked up, and we became silent, content to watch the rowdy roosting distraction and let our problems smolder away in a cognac-scented haze.

A roadrunner and javelina sometimes scurried past or snorted in the distance. When it turned dusk, the coyotes would scream, and I would try not to. With the sunset fading behind a mountain or a bright moon illuminating the crisp, arid night, we would discuss the classes we were struggling to pass, the room-mates we were deciding to avoid, and what the hell to do with our lives after graduating. Despite our pursuit of self-improve-ment through higher education, we struggled to comprehend how our cargo pants and 3D puzzle remnants of the analog era-defining past would fit in an unknown future beyond term papers and fast food, *somewhere else.*

WITH RECENTLY PURCHASED two-way radios clicked on and a suitable variety of high-calorie snacks on board, the trip's execu-tion was as creative as its official justification. We sold the expe-dition to our parents as a "transportation necessity" to fulfill summer jobs back east. In reality, the only criteria influencing our decision-making that vindicated the trip were the following: (1) exhibited a sense of adventure, and (2) required many hotels.

Except for a brief hiccup in New Mexico, we accomplished

the rally uneventfully within a week, went our separate ways to pursue temporary summer jobs, and carelessly ran up the minutes on our parents' cellphone plans for two months. We reunited again at school in mid-August with new flip phones, fresh haircuts, and a vow rivaling the conviction and passion of the *Titanic*'s Jack and Rose—but with the faint soundtrack of the White Stripes' Jack and Meg playing through tinny Ranger speakers—to never put that much distance or time between the two of us ever again.

I wish the cross-country journey had transpired without incident and was the beginning of a heartwarming memoir highlighting our financial struggles, but that would be as fictitious as cable TV programming masquerading as "history." The real reason to continue writing, though, is that I have a railroad track of stitches holding my back together; because real life can be plot-twisting and heart-wrenching as double VHS tapes of Hollywood's interpretation of a cruise line tragedy. Thank God microsurgery has advanced alongside CGI and data storage since the '90s, or I'd be as helpful as a VCR is to Generation Z.

Besides, with temporary mobility restrictions and a current sick-leave status, what else am I supposed to do?

THE NEW MEXICO hiccup should be on record. It was an abrupt detour, and the first actual warning I should have heeded about the villains chasing my ass. I was pushing the speed limit by fairly conservative rule-breaking standards and employing the measures any seasoned interstate traveling driver would, such as frantically braking the instant the flashing red lights lit up my rearview mirror. After a brief delay in judgment, I pulled over, watching the little pickup I was supposed to be following do the same, a few hundred feet in the now less opportunistic future.

I fumbled for the glove box and grabbed the registration, my eyes darting up to the self-dimming luxury mirror that was always too dim, watching two shaved tan heads with hats and sunglasses talking to each other in their dusty Crown Vic. One cop finally moved and strolled alongside the Lincoln, taking as much time as a dial-up modem and touching the taillight before reaching the open passenger window.

The officer was suspicious, peering through the passenger window before asking for the usual documentation.

I obliged.

"Can you step outside the car?" he inquired.

Of course, I'm not a felon—just an innocent student-pilot, future-government-spy badass, I thought, dropping the tinted aviator sunglasses into the cigarillo-stuffed ashtray and taking the key out of the ignition. I stood in front of the patrol car, trying to appear calm and in precise control of my soda-filled bladder, knowing full well I was going to be screwed. In retrospect, I think the law enforcement duo realized I was getting nervous, looking more like Nicolas Cage in *Raising Arizona* than someone innocent.

My eyes darted back to the blacked-out rear window, the beaming sun radiating off its chrome-trimmed frame. *Oh shit. I hope my leather jacket, or at least the Goldfish crackers, are hiding the open rum bottle on the rear seat. And where is the vodka? The trunk?*

"Some car. Must be *fast*," the officer announced.

I agreed with a reluctant, nervous laugh, but not without some counterproductive defenses: "Yeah, but I was keeping up with traffic on the highway" and "It's old, so it really isn't fast by today's standards."

"Well, it must be modified, right?"

"No, it's barely running."

The cop wasn't happy with these answers. His partner sat inside the cruiser, checking the computer for a suspected record, which didn't appear since I didn't have one, so both cops pursued the matter with a more aggressive barrage of questioning that went to the best of my terrified memory something like this:

Cop number 1: "So, you just painted the car?"

Cop number 2: "Yeah, that paint looks spotless."

"No, the clear coat is peeling."

Cop number 1: "Why do you have a knife on your belt?"

I forgot I did until now. Shit. "Are they illegal in this state?"

Cop number 2: "No, it's OK. But you must expect trouble?"

"No, why, uh ... should I?"

Cop number 1: "Oh, Mexicans? Are they a problem where you're from?"

"No."

Cop number 1: "This isn't Arizona, kid. *They've* got meth, right?"

Yeah, well, it's no Mayberry here either.

Cop number 2: "Who is the accomplice in the pickup truck? Girlfriend? *Boyfriend?*"

"Girlfriend." *Dick cop.*

Both cops stared at the now settled dust cloud, where the pickup sat crooked along the edge of the road.

Cop number 1: "Oh, is *she* expecting trouble?"

I guess I will die in a small-town jail, probably because of meth-ravaged inmates. Or maybe Mexicans. Great. I shouldn't have watched so much Top Gear *during my childhood. This never happens to those guys.*

The inquisition ended with a written warning and a fine that had me anxiously recalculate my gas budget. When our convoy resumed at the pace of your average hybrid car, I glanced up at the smoke-stained visor and laughed, not at the "airbag murdering you" warning, of course, but at the silver-colored emblem attached to the brim, which resembled an angel. These words were inscribed: *Don't drive faster than your guardian angel can fly.* I had left the amulet there from the previous owner in the same way you might leave a cross that was found in the cellar of an old house you had purchased in a creepy town. Some possessions unintentionally transfer from one party to another. If you have watched enough horror films *and* have lived in New England at any point in your life, you know not to make unnecessary changes unless you want to die in a sudden and tragic mystery that baffles local detectives.

The immediate lesson from this angelic warning was clear: Don't overestimate the speed of a guardian angel and don't trust the previous owner's claim that the car was "bone stock" except for the wheels. However, the more critical prophecy didn't surface until over a decade later, serving as a chilling premonition of misfortune. It was a devil's-in-the-details kind of thing I had overlooked in my zealous infatuation with a new set of incorrect wheels, which meant so much more than a simple speeding ticket.

I'd trade my current situation for a million tickets or even premature baldness.

That old, long-haired, balding Italian transplanted in the Arizona desert, who desperately needed two grand for overwhelming medical expenses, never sat in the car when we looked at it and also couldn't drive it anymore. He announced with a convincing limp that he suffered from a bad back. My recent diagnosis revealed a similar prognosis; maybe it's my turn to be reckless and understate the facts.

ALL VILLAINS HAVE AN ORIGIN, and the white whale we rescued from an automobile graveyard run by a crypt keeper was no exception. The house with the neglected Lincoln sleeping in the driveway sat on the end of a street in a ranch-style development on the edge of a town the locals referred to as "meth valley." I guess we were stupid or brave before I could grow a "real" beard because I remember exiting the Ranger and thinking of abandoning the mission more than once. We cautiously walked past another Lincoln to get to the one for sale. It was love at first sight, I think.

The Lincoln was rare and not a popular choice; it was the car you'd expect a gangster to drive in an indie film from the early '90s that no one remembers. By the time they arrived on the used market, they had remained forgotten and cheap—if they hadn't already transitioned into a "hooptie" the instant the lease was up. Since WWII, the spare tire hump may have overstayed its welcome, diminishing any appeal to anyone born after the Craisin versus raisin war of 1989. Still, it was undeniably classy driving that car around even if an aftermarket CD player had replaced the original cassette.

It inspired the confidence that made you want to crank up some classic rock, wear a fedora, slick your hair back, and start smoking a cigar because the car came standard with a dedicated lighter and ashtray for every occupant. They are not worth their weight in scrap metal these days, though, which shows how rare things don't always translate to value.

"She runs great. Just needs to be tuned up." The tobacco aficionado waved his bony hand and wafting cigarette in the air with the eloquence of a conductor. His words, though, seemed to defy his actions. "I never smoked in it. Real clean. It's in good shape, although the speakers only work in the back."

I was staring at the inches of dust resting on the dash and a sooty film covering the steering wheel, wondering if the air freshener hanging from the mirror was supposed to be that color.

"Never smoked it in, kid," the owner continued, trying to change the subject. "What are you anyway, probably kissing 25, eh?"

"No, I'm 20."

"Oh, yeah, just what I thought," he nodded with confidence, one feeble hand to his "bad back."

"How's the transmission?"

"Oh, those mufflers should be replaced, and get rid of those cats. They're holding her back, you know. Slowing her down." He grabbed another cigarette that was hiding behind his ear.

Catalytic converters are unrelated to the transmission. "How're the brakes?"

"We put some Tiger Paws on her. Don't they look great with all the white lettering?"

Tires have nothing to do with brakes. This is going to be fun.

I glanced over at Michelle, who was studying the dirty car with new tires and a popping, leaky exhaust, and back to the lanky smoking salesperson, all hunched and as wiry as a cartoon villain. He was pacing around the driveway while narrating the noble life of the Lincoln, suggesting he was once spry.

"Yeah, we thought these wheels looked better than the original sport wheels."

That's a shame. Probably traded those for cigarettes, idiot. "You think it would make it across the country?"

"Oh sure, kid. I'd drive it anywhere right now. Just maybe take those cats off first. I know a guy who'll do that for you."

"It runs nice. Any oil leaks?

"She runs like a top. I don't want to see her go. I just need some money for my daughter who lives with us. Medical bills. Bastards just keep billing us."

"Oh, yeah." I shook my head to agree, but I had no clue about medical bills and suspected a meth habit was more likely. "Can you drop the price a little?"

His head indicated no, and he seemed insulted but was quick to counteroffer. "You like vinyl? I'll trade some vinyl."

I bet you'd trade anything, even your daughter. "No, I don't have any vinyl."

Michelle and I walked that day, but I couldn't let the prospect of owning that car go. We returned a week later with a stack of Benjamins to rescue the unloved Lincoln.

What a mistake.

So, yeah, the wolf disguised as a sheep so that it could kill other sheep was the title-loaned Lincoln. I should have scratched the sun-bleached sheet metal with the suspicious, oversize knife on my belt to see if black was hiding underneath the white paint. The love child of those infamous Hollywood B-movie "possessed but I'll love them anyway" cars. My first ticket to the bad-luck club and my first trip to AAMCO for a transmission rebuild. Perhaps, though (and more appropriate for this desert setting), it was a reincarnated fire-breathing and rabid-plagued javelina escaped from hell. Theatrical speculation aside, the car was as cursed as Jerome, Arizona, and, for the official record, I am exposing the cursed Lincoln's arrival into my life as *villain number one*.

HOSPITAL IN BOSTON
TWO CLOSE CALLS

JUNE 2021

THE DAY of the surgery was as miserable as the weather, but the doctors in Boston must know what they're doing because they knocked me out with something far more potent than Pineapple Express. The symbolic rain and unseasonably cold June hinted at dreary, unusual circumstances. However, I wasn't enjoying or commenting on the deluge because they forced my eyes shut for most of the day. You could say I was taking a coffee nap, minus the coffee, or a voluntary comforting afternoon slumber with an operating table replacing a couch. I immediately missed our sofa and the nearby aloe plant, which reminded me of serene cactuses inhabiting a less stressful place: a desert that now seems much nicer than this *somewhere else*. For all I knew, aliens had abducted me the second someone said I was "going to feel tipsy and tired," but I don't have any concrete proof. I was more likely taking part in some sick, hybrid version of Operation and Battleship for a solid 10 hours, and since I woke up again, I guess I won.

That round, anyway.

Waking up in the ICU, I embodied a doomed maritime

vessel, my immediate post-surgery condition rivaling even the most protracted Monopoly marathons I engaged in as a kid, though the villains rigged the game this time for sure. Not that I had a choice in the matter, any Goldfish crackers, or homemade iced tea nearby, but at least I wasn't alone. My support group turned nomadic ensemble wandered around in a daze, praying and upset, hoping a skillful surgeon would disband the villains. After being escorted from the chapel (their efforts to evade detection failed quickly), the displaced trio remained outside the hospital among the stoned and homeless people of Boston's Longwood Medical Area. There was even a shooting nearby that day. Amid this city drama, they monitored an app giving updates on my status, like at an airport, having no choice but to provide moral support remotely.

Someone may as well have banished them to the remote depths of the town at the bottom of the Grand Canyon called Supai.

But they were *here*, and that's all that really mattered.

JULY 1990

THIS WASN'T MY FIRST extended hospital visit or medical emergency, but it's the first I can remember. My family had informed me that my earliest near-death experience occurred not long after birth, before the "electronic skip protection" button showed up on CD players, when I almost went to heaven at 6 weeks old. I was too young to recall the weather or reminisce about the traumatic event, presumably also too young to have sinned (so I'd like to assume I was going to heaven). My heart skipped a beat or two, revving up to a high and unsafe rpm, turning me red and upset. After dropping the clutch a few times at stoplights when first acquainted with my wife's finicky pickup truck, I know the feeling. It was terrifying for everyone.

My mom said it was the scariest moment of her life, seeing me swell up as if I was being poisoned. Despite her parenting inexperience, she hastily drove to the doctor's office with the urgency of a race car driver, who told her to go to the emergency room, where they submerged my head in ice. At first, this tactic worked, but unfortunately, there was an untimely sequel. I remained stable for a short time, but my rogue and frantic heartbeat escalated quickly. My mom told the specialists, who repeated the legal waterboarding method. Maybe that's why I never enjoyed swimming pools or being submerged in bathtub water or enlisted for a tour in Iraq?

I love iced coffee, though. How strange.

Although I do not know how conventional this technique was, if it was as popular as OPEC or "trickle-down economics," it saved my life and brought my redlining heart rate back to acceptable levels. They monitored and medicated me for the following year before the doctors advised a reluctant mom to let me live a normal lifestyle, clearing my rebellious juvenile heart. The only dietary restriction was caffeine and chocolate, which I now half ignore because coffee is a vessel for the *real* "magic molecule"—$C_8H_{10}N_4O_2$—an excellent legal drug gifted to us by the Divine, the Arabica gods, or maybe some guy working in a lab.

The doctors encouraged my mom to hand over the keys to the proverbial helicopter some parents have idling on standby, ready to pilot whenever their child eats dirt or falls. I caught a lucky break and outgrew the condition, lived a healthy and uneventful sugar-free childhood, evading any real villains for nearly three decades.

Until now, when dealt another bad hand at a casino I don't recall walking into.

I'M NOT USUALLY a sucker for nostalgia until I step inside a casino. It's on par with rediscovering a past world that somehow evades mainstream ordinances and "cancellation enthusiasts." Though the cast of characters inside usually appear to be one precarious sip and puff away from death. It brings to mind what the West's ghost towns were like before folding up when the mines or wells ran dry. But in all honesty, we have little discretionary income, no "backer," and a lot of skepticism toward the virtues of the lottery. Besides, Michelle and I are also indisputable bad-luck magnets. These are not redeeming qualities in a gambling establishment, so the chance of us being inside one is very rare.

We only frequent casinos when a comedian or band performs at the venue, because gambling is a scam. That's my excuse to eat a few doughnuts when the Hot Light beckons with the same mesmerizing seduction as the light refraction phenomenon found in the desert known as a mirage. The sugar high, though, is no mirage. It's as real as the crash I experience 20 minutes later when I'm fighting the urge to take a coffee nap, often craving that cult burger chain that exists only on the "other" coast, with Bible verses stamped on the bottom of the cups. Besides fresh doughnuts and getting trapped between long-legged girls with cocktail trays, the only appeal a casino has is being reminded how the '90s diner experience included a similar pungency. That was before mandated bans on indoor smoking, when I started spiking my hair and claiming a free personal-pan pizza for reading books (not that I needed such an incentive to devour literature). Although I abstained from games of chance and did my best to stash the Cheerios Sacagawea coins and paper savings bonds that fell out of birthday cards in those deep cargo-pants pockets, maybe I should've practiced shuffling playing cards instead of shuffling to multiple jobs after school so that I could one day buy a hot-rod Lincoln.

Money isn't everything, and I guess I subscribe to a popular prevailing concept that experiences are more valuable than possessions. Perhaps that's why I forget the outside world and all the problems attached to it when I'm chewing coal-fired pizza, counting the doughnuts on the conveyor belt, and marveling at the walking dead wheezing and migrating from one venue to the next when I'm struggling to find fresh air in casino land. Casinos also remind me of the outlaws in the Wild West films we binge-watched as kids, and why I'll start thinking of those VHS tapes or the thrilling childhood memories of a trip to any of the now-defunct video rental stores. That's when our parents allowed us to pick only one new-release movie to add to our fat stack of older films during the weekly excursion to Hollywood Video or Blockbuster. These movies were "a few dollars more" and sometimes unavailable because of popular demand, especially if they were too exhaustive to fit on one cassette.

Maybe everything *was* better before 2010?

If my luck had run out before I started paying taxes or before non-interest-accruing savings accounts existed, I presumably would have depleted the hollowed-out book stuffed with $20 bills on a used Mitsubishi 3000 GT. I think Michelle would have either approved or buried me with a spade, but it sounds like buying a house around the 2008 implosion meant the bank asked for your name and not much else. Not that we were even thinking of joining the first-time homeowners' club, because renting was cheaper than owning and Zillow wasn't yet a household name. I was perhaps still fantasizing about Fox Body Mustangs and future careers. Our biggest challenge was figuring out whose parent to get to cosign the apartment lease, even though I hadn't bought a diamond ring yet because completing a degree seemed more critical.

Those challenges now seem petty. Funny how perspective changes everything.

Since everything's gone to shit since I was an adult out of college, I might as well see if the Texas Hold'em app I played a decade ago during class even exists. Of course, I could find out how late the local casino is open, but with my horrible luck, my savings will dissipate quicker than the bottle of rum did the day I turned 21. It wouldn't surprise me if I draw the Ace of Spades 10 seconds after sitting my sorry ass down at a blackjack table, and naturally, a lightning bolt will strike my heart.

Perhaps reminiscing is just spinning tires in the mud. I did that once as a kid on a farm when misjudging a field after heavy rain, convinced four-wheel drive wasn't necessary. Obsessing about the past is probably just as bad as digging deeper into some hopeless, dismal situation, remaining stuck or unproductive. I try to stay optimistic and forward-thinking because treading water is what I had trouble doing during ocean swims, and besides, I'm as much a swimmer as a gambler, and now I kind of miss working on a farm.

THEY SAY my 10-year outlook is promising. So, I have that going for me. The doctors also believe about 10 years ago, the villains showed up, right about when I was happily cruising around with a lovely Boston girl in an unlucky Lincoln. How times have changed. The reason I returned to the hospital after such a long hiatus seems surreal, a complete shock, and much worse than an ill-timed bet, rewinding a VHS, or even a run-in with New Mexican Barney Fife. This time my fear-filled bladder wasn't full of soda, but since the catheter took care of the inevitable outcome, I couldn't even piss my pants. Not that I was wearing any anyway.

VILLAIN NUMBER 2: THE COMMUTE

MAY 2013

THEY ADDRESSED our bills to a Virginia town called Manassas, but some clever locals merged a syllable to produce something worse: Ma-nasty. Living in an apartment complex where cars were spray-painted in the parking lot overnight only augmented this tainted reputation and had me double-checking the deadbolt at night. The studio apartment was spartan and made hauling a mattress up the stairs challenging because it was on the third floor, which seemed important even though it was the least of our problems. The lease was cheap, and we were chasing the most affordable rent because we were credit-poor and cash-strapped, despite merging our finances.

The evening was the best part of the day because I wasn't sitting in traffic anymore, enraged from adjusting the seat's height, distance, tilt angle, and headrest, trying to find some holy grail configuration that might finally feel comfortable. Five days out of seven, I figured out dinner alone by opening a can of something while drinking canned beer, having returned home earlier than Michelle and believing "cans" somehow accommodated a tight budget. I started work insanely early courtesy of insane traffic caused by Quantico and Eisenhower's accurate prediction of a military-industrial complex.

It was around 6:15 p.m. when Michelle opened the door to find the disaster I had created. I'm lucky she didn't turn around and "trit-trot to Boston" because they train the local children to do that from birth.

"What smells like, uh, pretzels?" she asked, kicking off her new cowboy boots. She now sold them for some Great Recession era reason.

"I'm sorry. I tried!" Rising from behind the kitchen island counter, I wheeled around from the opened 400-degree oven.

Her ordinarily calm heart-shaped face expressed alarm. She looked red, and her eyes blinked as rapidly as the light of the smoke detector I had smothered with a pillow moments before because the blaring saucer wouldn't shut up.

"I tried to surprise you with something nice, and I messed up!"

I raised a spatula in one hand and the singed pot holder in the other. Both gestures probably spoke louder than my explanation. I turned back to the oven to rescue a burned cookie wedged in the crack between the door hinge that seemed as sticky as prickly pear cactus candy.

Michelle did not notice the crispy, well-done chocolate chip cookies oozing lava onto the floor, distracted by my dramatic cookie rescue extraction methods.

"Ugh! I burned the fabric on the barstool!" This confession was bitter and accompanied by waving the blackened hockey puck around while pointing to a baking sheet of similar black discs.

"Oh wow, you made cookies. That's awesome." Her confidence was not guileless or sarcastic; exhaustion was taking its toll.

"No! I burned them. They're terrible."

I glared at the black half of a checker set on the counter, infuriated that my plan to make something to sugarcoat a bad time in this lousy shithole, had backfired. I reached to grab the charred pan, getting burned through the glove, and threw the baking sheet on the counter. The cookies that flew off resembled poker chips, and one landed on the fabric chair that used to be tan.

She laughed at the branded stool cushion, presumably because it was funnier than our hopeless attempts to survive as adults drowning in debt. "Guess we are not getting our deposit back ... maybe you could work on a ranch branding cattle?"

The thought of ranching out west seemed appealing, but it didn't hide my outrage. I tried to remain as taciturn as Rooster Cogburn. Still, I probably sounded more like Katharine Hepburn with a trace of a suppressed Jersey accent, clutching some ice to my "hot hand" that seemed as unlucky as the sound editor was for the sequel to *True Grit*. We were far from hitting any kind of jackpot, and I wanted to hit my head against the wall. But the drywall seemed too thin, and I may have hated our situation more than the lack of subtitles in the remake despite Jeff Bridges' gravelly drawl. The apartment made our college dorm rooms look big, and the mattress I loathed almost shared the kitchen.

Don't worry. We will move out of here soon. Maybe I'll fake my death, ditch student loans and government bureaucracy, run away somewhere the debt collectors and cockroach-infested boot store owners won't find us. Perhaps somewhere in Maricopa County, where we'll set up a ranch or at least eat some salad with ranch dressing and order an authentic Neapolitan pie. I really miss bianco-style pizza.

I repeated a familiar mantra. "But first, let's get rid of that mattress. It's killing my back."

THE SEARCH for a simple mattress started when I graduated college and was ready to embark on my first post-degree career in Northern Virginia. I arrived in the state proclaiming to be for lovers upon graduating in 2011, leaving Arizona the same year the International UFO Congress moved to Phoenix. Go figure; I should've stuck around, studied something as scientific and profitable as ufology instead of the pilot and spy shit. The mattress quest began at a famous wholesale "club" that arranged their sleeping products like a bunch of oversized CDs or vinyl in a record store before the internet pirates gutted the industry. They were all stacked on their sides and looked the same except for sizes probably selected by bored marketing associates. In those days, my mattress knowledge was as minimal as our apartment, which was as hospitable as Nothing, Arizona.

Memory foam, gel, latex, pocketed coil, conventional coil, adjustable, heating, cooling, hemp, straw, or a "hybrid" of all these ordinary and exotic materials: Mattresses are more diverse than urgent care waiting rooms, spanning many possibilities and combinations tailored to every human back possible. They even design them for dogs and possibly cats because people have too much Bitcoin these days.

I grew up in modest, shared rooms with small accommodations, beginning with a crib and eventually a bunk bed. I graduated to something marginally more extended than a twin with a desk underneath for ultimate space-saving frugality in college. Ironically, my student loan debt does not reflect frugality. You'd think I lived in a five-star hotel for years like a trust fund kid who drove a German sedan with functional electronics and brakes. Now that I was expecting a great future career and my girlfriend living with me after she graduated, it was time to upgrade to a larger, more spacious mattress. For some reason, I chose the "traditional spring." I felt somewhat traditional. The Lincoln had undergone conversion to a spring suspension, which was comfortable, and the discount club seemed sensibly priced.

I had no second thoughts about the purchase until we spent a few months getting used to it. Or, *putting up with it*, I should say. When I would get up in the morning, my back ached. I initially assumed I was unwittingly karate-kicked at night by a companion who secretly took Judo, or perhaps by hostile ninjas who vanished whenever I woke up. It didn't hurt per se, just ached a little. Maybe I was getting old, now well into my 20s. The future didn't look like it would get more comfortable as I aged, so the least I could do was get the best mattress possible.

ONE EARLY FOGGY MORNING, the sad red economy sedan barreled down a pitch-black Virginian road, attempting to set a new time trial record. Life was stressful and the road was a little sandy. The mismatched tires were bald, and my judgment wasn't as good as it would be in the future. These elements combined were the perfect recipe for inevitable failure; it was only a matter of when an accident would happen. The car performed the signature "Jersey power slide" maneuver I had a bad habit of implementing during hairpin turns.

This time, though, it was too late. I collided with a boulder hiding around a blind curve and had no drift or speed boost button to correct my mistake.

Bang! The impact was abrupt and loud as I forced the brake pedal to contact the floor. I may have closed my eyes for a split second, worried the commute had sent me to the hotel in heaven, and I didn't even know if I had a reservation because I'm sure there's an app for that. I didn't even have a smartphone, because we were involuntarily thrifty. The drifting red missile somehow bounced off the giant boulder and came to a sliding stop before I hit more rocks lined up at the edge of this long driveway because the homeowner didn't want his perfect lawn to get ruined. I thought I could go faster than physics would allow. That theory proved a more significant mistake than purchasing the 90,000-mile underpowered "hooptie" with cracked or missing hubcaps and a worrisome transmission chirp.

Thanks a lot, Lincoln.

I hated making unwise purchases, but the jinxed Lincoln's

brakes had crapped out, and parts were impossible to find. The mechanics became amused, the car enthusiasts preachy: "Shoulda bought the Mustang, kid. Fox Body Mustang. Plenty-a-parts, almost the same car, you know. Just easier to get parts," they advised, a few hundred times. The forums seemed to agree, and I'm not sure if I needed to dump the right magic potion into the gas tank and it would've turned into a better car, but it was the unpopular jalopy I was stuck with. Sadly, though, it couldn't withstand the abuse of the rigorous Beltway commute.

Driving around with an additional problem every week was expensive. I wasn't profiting from automotive calamities, so I needed a reliable vehicle, without all the quirks and cursed baggage rolling around in the solid "two-body" trunk. However, we didn't have any spare cash or an open line of credit at the "Bank of Mom and Dad." Our credit scores were as dismal as the eligible vehicle choices we faced, and an undesirable outcome seemed the only 100 percent guarantee. After several mainte-nance visits, I questioned whether the Lincoln was tempera-mental and only enjoyed Arizona roads. In that state, the car ran faster than a roadrunner. If I had been driving a low-riding white lightning coupe along the Virginian twisty, I could've avoided the crashing part, I think.

The accident reminded me of a similar regrettable vehicular antic along a winding and desolate road on the edge of Skull Valley. Luckily, the cursed Lincoln had better tires and a generous helping of buttery smooth torque than the red sedan, and I powered out of that misjudged maneuver with reckless abandon. This was critical because the rocks hugging those Arizona roads were more significant than in Virginia, before the terrain transformed into a lush pastoral scene. When that scene abruptly ended, there was a graveyard and a small Mormon church whose parking lot I used to perform U-turns because the gas gauge on the white whale was as reliable as my 2G phone signal. It's also possible I was scared of being stranded in a valley suspiciously named after skulls, despite my recurring fascination with driving to that scenic location.

Although I treated the red sedan like a rally car because I was either optimistic or hopelessly delusional, it wouldn't die. The sad vehicle lost another hubcap and suffered a small dent on the passenger door, but that was the extent of the visible damage. It seemed too good to be true, and I resumed my race to work by adopting a caution lap approach, convinced my accident should have been much worse and that maybe my amateur stunt-car-driver antics were unhealthy.

MY TYPICAL WORKDAY began with budget-brewed Arabica beans, black and bold and unpolluted. After running down the stairs and getting into the economy hatchback with a bluish tint, resembling sparkle toothpaste, that replaced the red sedan, I locked the door out of habit. The coarse idling car purred louder than the cat who would sometimes sleep underneath it (I was somehow a magnet for cats).

Maybe it was my confidence or good looks; I don't really know that much about cats.

The pitch-black parking lot this early was desolate and cat-infested, but I ignored the bleak surroundings and nocturnal traffic as much as possible. I fumbled with my phone, the tangled government ID lanyard, and the car's climate control, hoping the coffee would kick in. There was no time for warming the car up, so if it was cold, I borrowed a coworker's horrible advice and revved up the soda-bottle-sized engine before snapping the manufacturer-recalled dual-clutch transmission hastily into drive.

I have lousy transmission luck, or just all-around bad luck.

Perhaps that explains the cats?

As usual, regardless of subjective and debatable "luck," I pushed forward. If everything went as planned, I would succeed in the ultimate race against time: *the commute.* I can sadly attest, the "Mixing Bowl" and nearby Interstate 95 are notorious for some of the worst traffic jams in the Northeast. My commute varied every year, as did our address. Neither was enviable, though, since we were poor yet somehow "middle class." However, it didn't matter where we lived. My slow-motion, mile-marker-counting migration was always a mix of psychologically and physically draining exercises, as creative as the Obamacare legislation Congress was fighting over.

Sitting for hours in bumper-to-bumper traffic over an extended duration will change a person, but not in a productive way leading to enlightenment. All radio stations eventually sound dreadful, and the bad news seems somewhat reasonable. Cringeworthy habits seem to develop overnight. Shameful and aggressive thoughts consume the mind. You recognize everyone else on the interstate as you chomp on sticks of gum or light up to relieve stress. After months or years, you'll wave or nod your head to strangers because you see them more than anyone else. There's something sad yet reassuring in acknowledging collective regrettable decision-making as if to announce, "Yeah, we both must've made a big mistake to be riding out the same awful thing." There was even a particular element of camaraderie, like, "Oh good, we both avoided that pile of broken glass from the last pileup the faint radio voice was telling us killed a few people. How many MPGs are you getting, bro?"

Clutching the steering wheel, seething at minivans and hybrid cars that leave gaps between traffic with their stick family or environmental pledge advertised on the rear window, can weigh on your psyche. Pretty soon, passive irritation turns to active rage, causing questionable swerving and unprovoked challenges between you and all the zombie drivers. There is a tendency to floor the gas pedal at every brief, open stretch of the roadway before warping the brake rotors. When the drag strip runs out, so does your sanity. Accidents make matters worse but provide some sick form of gladiator-rivaling distraction from the surrounding idiots crawling through traffic. Those involved seem content to shorten their lives to pursue a career they bitch about when they arrive home hours late, assuming the motorist zombies arrive unscathed from the villainous commute and if they even bother going home anymore. Seedy motels halfway to home look good after a while, despite the roaches.

Passing through a maze of security checkpoints and parking in a crowded garage, I swiped and displayed my security badge a million times before sitting in front of a computer screen to stare at satellite imagery. I was ecstatic, now living the vague and distant "adult dream" as the wholly realized government-employed white-collar badass I envisioned for myself in college.

Just kidding. Now I know not everything is what it seems.

CELEBRITIES AND SCREENWRITERS are scamming us all anyway; they may just be former used-car sale associates who ran away to restart their lives in Hollywood. Washington, DC, is a series of clusters and not the good kind you find in a cereal box or a galaxy. The spy thrillers ignore traffic jams, Beltway mayhem, and the infuriating tedium of desk jobs. None of these mundane realities are even remotely as interesting as moles, double agents, and Russian redhead honeypot spies whispering over lattes in artsy cafés trying to solve elaborate puzzles while obscured by vape smoke and mirrors. Even though I was there for less than three years, I knew there must be something less monotonous than developing acute carpal tunnel syndrome from scrolling with a mouse all day and being forced to wear two-inch-thick glasses due to staring at screens. I contemplated a future less dismal than illegally racing down the HOV lane and scarfing energy nut cluster bars every morning, having no time for a real breakfast and no money for eating out.

I would glare at the analog clock at work throughout the day, ruminating on all our financial challenges, hoping someone would interrupt the thought loops by suggesting "coffee time." When that was over, it was back to the classified vault to work on developing computer vision syndrome, wondering if I should eat the frugal peanut butter sandwich that sat on my desk or be reckless and gamble lunch at the government's answer to a food court. I didn't have to make a bet to find out if I had good or bad luck, but the peanut butter wasn't that much better either, and I kind of wished a seagull would show up and steal it. My only saving grace was that I still had my health and somehow my girlfriend, despite habitual prepackaged foil-wrapped breakfasts and bittersweet job-security prospects. Michelle stuck around even though employment opportunities were a string of retail and food service gigs she was overqualified for, somehow providing little more than a hysterically mediocre paycheck.

That was when the adversity *really* began. I realized one of my biweekly paychecks covered the rent, the other covered student loans, and we were shit out of luck for the rest of the expenses. During that difficult time, I received plenty of wise advice, including "Shoulda went to trade school. Shoulda gone to community college. Shoulda worked harder through school. Shoulda just not gone to school if you couldn't afford it. Isn't that what the military is for?" That was always as helpful as saying, "Shoulda been born into a rich, Oxford-educated, family with a team of advisers charting my life from birth to guarantee success."

I know this narrative hasn't delved into uncharted territory, and our challenges weren't anything unique or an isolated struggle. Everyone seems to know someone attempting to overcome burdensome education expenses or pitiful entry-level pay scales. However, it was the one glaring six-figure elephant in the room trying to smother us, an insurmountable obstacle. Now, I realize it doesn't matter whether I'm remorseful for being educated, since I'm sure degrees are as overrated as any electronic device with an apple stamped on it. So, yeah, I fell for the scam that a degree "pays off," but make no mistake, this is no apology for pursuing an education.

Some of us have a "bad back" and can't move rocks around all day.

However, that didn't stop me from ever working (despite the villain's best efforts). Go figure. I never claimed unemployment benefits or received one of those recurring supplements the COVID bailout sent to people for sitting on their asses or cranking out more kids. It's some kind of stiletto dropkick in the teeth that the Department of Education doesn't count the fucking U.S. Intelligence Community or the U.S. Postal Service as government employers eligible for student loan forgiveness. I don't know how good the screen actors' retirement and educational benefits are, but maybe I should've left and limped the Lincoln away to California.

Could have been a stunt driver. Probably be wealthy, semifamous B-list actor. I've been told I have a handsome face, in spite of childhood acne resembling a Biblical plague.

Pretentious sarcasm cloaked as wisdom aside, all I know is whether you are a tradesperson, CEO, burrito roller, or homeless bum, it doesn't matter one fucking cent to the man upstairs or whoever the villains work for. When your health is in jeopardy, it is of little consequence if you dropped out of second grade or completed a second master's degree. The MRI doesn't care if you choose to drive or walk to work because of environmental pollutants and lithium mines. You're still going to be just as screwed and pondering the fragility of life when death whispers in your ear. Odds are you're going to wind up in the same type of box in the same ground as some prick with a Napoleon complex who ditched ex-wives and responsibilities, yet garnered tons of social media popularity.

Death seems the only way to get student loan forgiveness, and I'm not interested. The irony is my unexpected health crises only reinforced what I already knew: Health is more important than wealth, and it sucks when you don't have either.

POLITICS UNDOUBTEDLY FUELS a toxic cloud of angst. Northern Virginia is just as polluted, drowning in a sea of corruption and conceit. It was challenging to breathe literally and figuratively after experiencing the much superior, arid utopian Arizonian desert's unrestrained lifestyle, and we regretted ever leaving. Despite the smoggy negativity we tried to trudge through the mounting adversity and stress, hoping it would somehow pay off one day. Besides, all the adults in my early life only told me "go to school, kid" so that you don't wind up poor and pensionless.

That advice proved misguided, outdated, and as helpful as a 100-pound cinder block chained to your leg the second a diploma hits your hand.

I packed my lunch in a paper bag, skipped the dentist for years, and could barely afford a haircut, which may be why I grew it out and was told I resembled various celebrities. I did my best to brush off the plaque and resemblance comparisons because that didn't get me any closer to being debt-free. Michelle cut my hair once in the tiny space where the kitchen, living room, and bedroom joined but had trouble trimming my neckline and trimmed a mole instead. The horror on my face and the guilt on her face when we both ran to the bathroom mirror was more unsettling than the bloody electric razor she was wielding. I'm lucky that I didn't faint because the sight of blood has that effect, especially when it's dripping down my neck.

WE MAY HAVE PONDERED TAKING a grace period from ourselves; after all, we were not violent people or inclined to hold up a bank, and Michelle even swore off haircuts for years. But deferment seemed lonely, and we sure as hell had no desire to default. My soulmate and I loved each other too much, despite those botched, unintentional dermatology adventures, cramped living quarters, and stagnant student loan balances.

I spent almost as much time commuting as working and realized sitting all day at a desk staring at a black-and-white world was more miserable than cool. The career was mildly rewarding but more draining than a vampire orgy in *From Dusk till Dawn*. No matter how much frugality we exerted even the Netflix subscription would have to be cut, and then I'd go through Salma Hayek withdrawal. Life can be cruel. But at least I had my health, I remember reflecting, and Michelle, who was equally stressed and aloof.

I became so miserable that I started eyeing yellow packs of cigarettes at the gas station, yearning for drive-through liquor stores in the good ole Wild West of central-western Arizona. After exploring cash advances, refinancing, and student loan deferment options, we realized the future at our current salaries was unsustainable. The simple math told the story better than I could. We were drowning in liability and scared the grocery bill would run up the monthly tab to unpayable levels and drying the checking account the way Arizona's wells will be one day. Michelle and I shared a growing suspicion that they rigged everything in the house's favor, and since we couldn't play the game very well, we did the next best thing and became strippers. Just kidding. We counted cards. *Credit cards.*

WALKING side by side in haunted national parks, Michelle and I brainstormed. After graduating and struggling to transition to full-time working adult life in DC, we realized that humidity, bills, and student loans were too disenchanting. We soon gravitated to the Civil War battleground parks overrun with deer, mosquitoes, and unexplainable activity we guessed were ghosts. After all, admission was usually free, and the experience was the closest we could find to our Arizona hikes, minus the requisite Cinnamon Twists. Those desert excursions had accustomed us to scorpions, rattlesnakes, and the occasional wandering hippie who strayed too far from their mobile home park. Rural Virginia was comparatively tame.

Eventually, we began running because strolling through

historical battlegrounds became as depressing as a cruise around the neighborhoods surrounding Winslow's iconic corner. Sometimes speed creates a more exciting existence than the environment, not that running very fast was even possible with my sedentary lifestyle. Perhaps we were delusional victims of the notion that repetitive exertion would make us at least appear healthier. I once worked with a middle-aged guy who chomped on nicotine gum during the day, chain-smoked at night, and trained for marathons on the weekends. That was only when he experienced a dating dry spell. By his own admission, he didn't expect to live past 60, and the running kept him fit enough to score the next hot date. However, Michelle and I were a little more optimistic, being only a few ticks past 20 and 100 years of living somehow still seemed possible. We wanted to make the best of our time together, assuming that our bodies would ache less if we walked and ran through muggy swampland. Maybe we'd even last long enough to qualify to live in an off-grid trailer park commune tax haven, Arizona style. The running, however, was short-lived, and I couldn't wait to end the program.

I wish finding a great hiking trail or mattress was the biggest challenge we faced.

At the expense of a grating existence, the gratifying experiment in pursuing a dream job right out of college was as exciting as winning a life's supply of Ramen soup, minus the flavor packet. It seemed every week passed that I saw someone quit, retire, or die commuting. After three years, I decided I did not wish to become a casualty before being eligible to retire, so I quit. After all, "sitting," they claim, "is the new smoking," and after doing too much of both activities, my soulmate and I didn't want to do either in an overpriced, humid swamp. New England sounded refreshing, and a change of scenery seemed like what we needed to help us turn things around: *a restart.*

HOSPITAL IN BOSTON

MARBLES AND BOTANICALS

JUNE 2021

ON THE CUSP of the end of visiting hours, and as my former hot-girlfriend-turned-wife was about to leave the dim hospital room, I experienced a life-changing milestone. It occurred the very day I turned 31, shrouding a typically jovial occasion with a vertical cumulonimbus hail cloud that seemed to encapsulate what it means to hit rock bottom. With a horrifying unease at my environment, in between counting ceiling tiles and nurses, I embraced a glaring insomnia-induced epiphany, and I swear I wasn't three sheets to the wind. It was a sobering beacon of enlightenment staring back at me, as clear as the mirror hanging on the wall across the room. Everyone needs to pin their problems on a villain, and upon extensive caffeine-fueled introspection, I've identified several.

My terminal roommate-patient moaned incessantly behind a privacy curtain, wheezing, whooping, crying, and grunting unintelligible phrases. The poor walking skeleton was deaf and disgruntled, using a cane to flip the light switch on and off a few dozen times. At one point, all the strange guttural noises and shuffling around the other side of the room suddenly stopped.

His warbled vocal cords broke the silence abruptly, saying something that sounded like "My head is going to die."

I didn't want clarification or to find out what the hell the unsettling prediction meant. Leaning close to the nurse as she handed me another round of pills, I inquired if the tortured bald guy was mentally OK. She reassured me he was and I didn't have to whisper because he was deaf. He "checked out" the other night while a hospital employee watched him because the staff had similar suspicions. The patient had a history of self-harm, but he was very nice to everyone else. At least, that's what the nurse reassured me as she snapped open another oxycodone pill pack, dropping one into a cup with a few other pills.

Because variety is nice, I guess.

I remained far from reassured, scared out of my mind, distraught from the slurry of drugs and post-surgery anesthesia fog clouding my unfamiliar environment. Sorely missing Michelle when visiting hours ended, my disposition in the wretched hospital hotel—perhaps really just a staged asylum— remained as ominous as the murder of crows that visit our yard to eat the pears. I also missed the sound of 100-year-old floorboards, shrunken door jambs, creaky hinges, radiator pipes tapping against the walls, and the 20-pound mouse scurrying across the ceiling, pissed that there's not enough insulation to stay warm. Hospital sounds are a harsh reminder of inevitable death. Beautiful old-house sounds, however, survive for multiple generations. This realization somehow comforts me at night when I can't sleep because it's unclear if a nearsighted ghost is stumbling around the spare room or if the house is loud because of single-pane windows and climate fluctuations. My wife reassures me it's only the humidity, temperature, or maybe Lunar-induced anomalies.

I also missed the view of the botanical-themed shower curtain I peered at most days from the toilet, reminiscing about the Desert Botanical Garden in Phoenix. That fantasy is much better than dragging a mobile pole on wheels and a brain juice pouch attached to my back to the hospital bathroom, where I was determined to do my business unassisted. Even when everything is going to complete shit, taking one on your own is a great success; I just wished the view was better. Maybe I'm a spoiled snowflake, but a hospital crap is hell, and the struggle to keep the drain tube from getting tangled up quickly erodes morale.

Botanical gardens are probably what Eden resembled before the wretched snake captured Eve's ear, hospital bathrooms are one "help pull cord" from hell, and if I could strangle the forces responsible for all my grief and flush them straight to hell, I most surely would. In an aggravating state of existence, I recollected my fragmented thoughts, writing a hospital journal so that the world would know if my roommate (whom I dubbed "Mr. Marble's") murdered me before the villains did. He was worthy of the title, mainly because he sounded like someone eating and choking on marbles. Fucking disturbing. Perhaps the whole medical procedure would somehow fail. Without firsthand documentation, *who would know the difference?*

VILLAIN NUMBER 3: THE DAMN ICE DAMS

DECEMBER 2014

THE RESTART WAS MORE of a cold start, an excellent way to destroy an engine if you don't warm it up and race your car down the street like an idiot. I suppose Michelle and I were like abused engines, running rough by the time winter was half over, and no amount of warming up, double-layered socks, or mediocre fountain drinks made any positive difference. We really needed a glass-bottled Mexican Coke with the cane sugar and a better view than dirty snow and frozen milk in glass bottles. It's the climate's fault; I get it. New Englanders can't help being crass and cold.

If the climate and drinks were warmer and more affordable, we could have quenched our thirst for mild success and eradicated the mountains of road salt plastered to our frostbitten faces. I wasn't *trying* to eat the stuff; sometimes, it gets in your mouth, and it's not same salt they use for a margarita glass. This phenomenon usually occurs when marching through unplowed sidewalks with a heavy bundle of mail, right as some asshole Jeep driver with a host of unresolved complexes floors through the slush and honks the horn to be extra friendly. That's when your face gets pelted with snowy road slop, and it's not pleasant. Oh, New England, you are a cruel and beautiful reminder of why people moved west!

No wonder Ben Franklin ran away.

Benjamin Franklin adopted a pen name and left Boston for Philadelphia. I did the opposite, except for the Arizona residence and a brief three-year stint in DC. Still, discrepancies are as irrelevant as the national debt, proposing a turkey as the national bird, or figuring out who recommended daylight saving time. The point is, Ben showed up in Philly and bought thrice as much bread as he could've had in Boston with the same amount of coins. Sometimes that's a good enough reason to move. We should've set our GPS to Philly, because Boston doesn't have cheap, excellent bread, hoagie rolls, bagels, pretzels, water ice, or German food. The woods were infested with turkeys, and the people seemed to only care about ice cream and football. So, there were some compromises, for sure, and we both missed *not* having to change the clocks twice a year back in Arizona. But we were young and stupid; time seemed eternal.

The Massachusetts adventure began at the very end of 2014, and there was nothing funny about any of it, even when we hung up the new cat-themed calendar for 2015, circling every day that *didn't* snow. I had packed the economy hatchback as tight as a clown car with most of what we owned, arriving confident I was unprepared and unemployed just in time to spend Christmas with Michelle's family. My conviction was remarkable, considering the circumstances. I thought I could become a true New England-Ah if given a chance, even if my wardrobe was climatically inadequate. The car that had somehow survived the Beltway commute was bright blue, and some people liked to comment on its resemblance to an Easter egg. That wasn't the look I was going for; it reminded me more of a turquoise rock–themed clock from Arizona that my grand-parents gave us one year when I was a kid. Besides, the car's MPGs were great. However, I don't think anyone in Boston minds paying for fuel. But that goes to show how far the great can fall, and if you're not defined as upper class by the IRS or enjoy record snowfall events, you shouldn't be moving to Boston.

We arrived in Beantown with a little less in our checking account than the benevolent founding father left for both cities when he died. That doesn't mean we were as wealthy as the worldly author of *Poor Richard's Almanack*. We were broke. Our bank account was depleted, like Franklin's coffers after a voyage to Paris, minus his indulgence in wine and women. Although France has always been expensive, inflation is a more potent force than often credited. Reluctantly, we moved to a less humid suburb south of Boston because that was where Michelle was from. Hometown roots can be more powerful than inflation, gravity, and democracy combined. As my former "airsick" flight instructor told me when popping an Advil and holding a paper bag to his face, he planned to move to Chicago to follow his fiancée when the semester ended. "Follow the wife, bro, happy life."

He's probably a bartender now, but I'm just speculating.

We were still unmarried and the relocation gave us a chance to dig out of our student loan graves by enlisting as postal apprentices and ditching rent. Despite the debt snares and "help not wanted" hiring sentiment during the Obama years, we still possessed a few ounces of youthful gumption and a lingering trace of naivety. We were hoping the future held promise and that we could adapt to any environment as effortlessly as a desert-dwelling chuckwalla. After arriving in New England, I realized I was only digging myself out of record snow bluffs. I also nearly broke my back. The villains were mutating and becoming bellicose. If I knew what was good for me, I should have adopted a pseudonym like Ben Franklin's "Silence

Dogood," moved to France, and opened a P.O. box instead of forwarding my mail.

Restarting didn't seem to be that helpful. "This never happens," I was told again and again, "not since the blizzard of '78." It wasn't the first or last time I was told something was rare.

Do rare people, or regular people with rare problems, attract rare things?

———

THE CALM before the snowstorm was mild and I had a lot of time to reflect on past decision-making even though I kept busy selling Christmas trees at a small family-owned farm. I remember staring at the muddy rows of leaning dead trees, wondering how I had arrived at this low point. The early morning fog still draped over the outbuildings and festive decor. The lights were wrapped around poles, the fence surrounding the place was hazy, and I couldn't see the sign telling people it was a nursery. The crowds would show up anyway in December, which meant taking a hard-earned break from hot cocoa siesta time, eggnog, and "Santa smut" binging. Time to dust off the scarf, wool mittens, and hit up a real farm that sold natural living plants, having to explain to kids these days, "We don't just harvest solar energy and pot." When the vehicles and families rolled into the lot, you could sense the widespread, cheerful basking of comfortable, generational wealth and feel the pride of mastering a freshly lit gas fireplace.

"BALSAM OR FRASER?" TAKE YOUR PICK and figure out how tall your ceiling is because unless you want to take me home with you, I'm only guessing. To be honest, I didn't care once someone had peeled out of the sandy parking lot with a shrink-wrapped tree strapped to the top of the vintage Subaru or Volvo wagon. I'd tie or throw the tree into the back of the typically expensive wagon, SUV, or pickup truck and hope they forked over a few bucks from shallow designer pockets and ugly puffy vests. I was banking on the gratuities to help me buy the coffee I was pounding down to get through the hellish experience that ends the day before Santa squeezes his ass down the chimney.

The only thing that would make matters worse was a record-breaking blizzard or if I fell off of a roof. When the aftermath of the snowstorm was still being publicized on NECN, I recounted my terrifying, tumbling story to Michelle. Before the season was over, I wondered if office work and Beltway mayhem were that bad, curdled whole-milk hot cocoa being as unwelcome as traffic.

JANUARY 2015

SHIT GOT REAL UP HERE—*it's a wicked severe storm!* If you hear these words announced by someone engaged in a passionate sport-themed conversation near Boston, don't panic because you think you're not as prepared as a local. There's a procedure to follow when the storm's predicted to hit. If it's a true Nor-east-ah, every single person panics at the absolute last minute, as snowflakes hit the pavement and they're cranking up the defrost with the windows cracked open while trying to follow a hockey game on the radio.

Run to the supermarket as you would on a Sunday 10 minutes before the Patriots game kicks off and load up the carriage with a dozen of only two products—milk and bread— because that's all you need to survive when it snows in Boston. Drop the bundles in the trunk, blow through any red lights, and honk the horn at anyone in front of you who is afraid to pass the salt truck and plow brigade. Don't forget to stop for an extra "laaahge reg-u-lah" (cream and sugar) iced coffee one last time to hold you over in case the cafés are closed tomorrow morning because the electricity is out. Scream an explicative at someone if they deserve it, particularly if they are slowing you down or *not* driving something with four-wheel drive. When you get back home to unload the bread and dairy, push the windshield wipers up, and don't forget your iced coffee that will freeze in the cupholder overnight, courtesy of global warming.

If the power goes out, don't panic. Curse the team that beat any Boston team last week, month, or 10 years ago for this bad luck as you throw all the dairy from the fridge into the milk box outside. I guess if you're afraid to light the gas stove or don't have one, that's why you bought all the white bread you usually never buy. Bread is a valuable carb source to hold you over until the world reopens again. With any luck, you will survive the storm and not have to go to work the next day, but even if you do, it's presumably only a short walk past the living room where you have an office near the gym, so you'll probably be fine. Unless you deliver the mail or plow parking lots—then you'll be outside.

———

GRAIN SCOOPS MAKE perfect snow shovels. Dig a path to the chicken coop. Dig out for the oil guy, a great uncle, the mailman, milkman, and trashman. Buy an old Jeep with an old plow or a Bobcat to plow the driveway, and have at least one backup snowblower because they only don't start when you need them to start. Park inferior, rear-wheel-drive vehicles strategically so that you can exit the driveway instead of performing pirouettes every morning when the pavement refreezes, transforming into an outdoor ice rink. Wear ice cleats called crampons that look as stupid as they sound and are as good on the ice as a Zamboni but as bad as cross-country skis at the beach if you try to go anywhere else.

The snow chores were endless, and while catching my breath from all the shoveling, I stared at the dirty icicles turning into stalactites running down the sides of the stained house, mesmerized by the remarkable effects of a destructive winter and the integrity of early 1900s asbestos. The preceding year was almost over when I arrived in Boston, and the weather was so unseasonably warm when 2015 began, that I remember raking leaves without a coat on. Someone scammed me upon my arrival because the record-breaking started almost immediately, and the tragic outcome of my decision became apparent.

THE DICTIONARY DEFINES an ice dam as "an obstruction to the flow of a river caused by the flow of a glacier." If you don't live on a river in the winter, you probably won't have to worry, but the phenomenon can happen to old New England houses. The more snow piled on top of the roof, the worse it becomes, so you must remove the snow before it transforms into a glacier. Try using a long pole—if you can reach the roof—or climb onto the roof and use a shovel if you can. Smart people pay someone else to do it because it's unsafe or convince family members to do it because they are on vacation in Florida sipping margaritas on the beach, keeping score of a volleyball game after eating buffet dinners at four o'clock.

But that's just speculation; I don't know that much about Florida.

If you do nothing about these ice dams, the walls inside your house can become scenic urban waterfalls, and the cats may panic when the peeling lead paint lands on their "nests." You risk losing that Christmas card with a lottery ticket stuffed in it at the last minute by a thoughtful great uncle because Social Security gave everyone a raise, and you risk losing your life to save a roof.

If the roof wasn't a sheet of ice hidden underneath a few feet of snow, I might have had a chance. Still, since my bad luck has been formally established, it should come as no surprise I would fall. I slipped, quickly losing traction and gaining momentum. Cursing and clawing at the icy shingles, I unknowingly took part in an impromptu Olympic-style luge event. I'm sure it more closely resembled a scene out of a *Chevy Chase* movie, except I wasn't getting paid and no one was laughing. While falling off the house, I couldn't help but remember why I was here, in the land of icicles, frost heaves, frappes, and dropped r's. *Thanks a lot, Virginia.*

I closed my eyes, expecting the landing to be as painful as when I jumped from the top of the sliding board as a kid, every aching vertebra protesting. I opened my frosty eyelids to see that I was alive, staring at the cloudy sky in the classic snow-angel pose. When I took a few breaths, climbed out of my shallow snow grave, and walked away in disbelief that I was unharmed, I was very grateful we had not shoveled the porch. That saved my ass, for sure. My landing resembled the chalk outline they draw around a murdered body more than a snow angel, and I swore that was too close a call to repeat. I declined going back on the roof to battle the damn ice dams.

NOT LONG AFTER sliding off the roof, I received a complimentary "value" meal lunch, so it wasn't too bad, and nothing was shattered except for my confidence. I still avoid roofs and refuse to participate in high-altitude adrenaline-boosting events like zip-lining. If I want a good jolt, I'll let the French press brew a few extra minutes or add more grounds to the pour-over. I'll pass on intentionally jumping off or out of things unless it's a bed infested with a rogue tarantula or a reclusive jaguar.

I was relieved to live another day to shovel more snow because the clouds couldn't hold it anymore or forgot where Maine was. The thrilling snow-tumbling experience taught me not to succumb to coercion and avoid shoveling snow off anything except the ground. However, a few years later, I wondered if this was one of many back-related incidents that cumulatively ruined my back. Maybe I twisted on my way down, or it was that time I slipped on the icy sidewalk and landed on my tailbone. Nope, it couldn't be. The doctor reassured me the villains were the culprit. Villains.

This harsh freshman New England winter proved rugged and unforgiving. It suddenly made sense why so many elderly residents flocked to Florida to escape. I was second-guessing the decision to move to Boston, hesitant to keep applying for an "outside" job similar to Michelle's. She was busily freezing her ass off delivering mail to those bright orange buckets people planted near the edge of their driveways because the storms had buried mailboxes until spring. There was simply too much snow and nowhere left to shovel it.

IF AN ECONOMY HATCHBACK clown wagon was a terrible choice for Boston, then I didn't give a damn about learning from my mistakes. I promptly traded it the first summer after that historic winter for an even worse vehicle. Except for winter commutes, the new car was better in all other respects because it was faster, eventually louder, and two doors leaner than the bright blue egg. My morale improved at the prospect of forgetting about the time before Boston, where I had wasted a few years of my life treading water. The Easter egg was a constant reminder of that time, and when I traded it, I never looked back.

Perhaps I was too busy looking underneath the long, sleek hood of its replacement. Just as the hood paint started peeling, I noticed the differential leaking; the brakes were squealing, and its ongoing maintenance issues reissued some suppressed Lincoln-era nostalgia. But that was OK, I didn't mind a little shadetree mechanic work to distract me from compounding debt and rising interest rates. Insurmountable financial obligations are a depressing phenomenon that takes its toll on you after a while, but I kept thanking God that at least I had my wife and my health. I alway's tried to remain positive in the face of adversity, flirting with a breakdown but trudging along, anyway.

However, buying too many cars may be a symptom of overwhelming adversity. I don't know really, except the problems fueling my decisions seemed "bad" until 2021. Now they appear as forgettable as tasteless instant coffee or racing stripes.

The retro fastback coupe was the younger cool-kid descendent of the old cursed Lincoln that I loved to hate, reminding me of whom I bought it with, the lovely saguaro, and mesquite scenery framed by those long tinted windows. The brooding red Mustang was also rear-wheel drive and sounded nearly as quick, not because I replaced its white side stripe with black but because it was "tuned" and the exhaust was less restricted. *But, no, I didn't get rid of the "cats."* It was already a cop magnet with the damn things.

The quickly deteriorating "Rust-Stang" was another bad-luck magnet, proven when a stoned old guy in a pickup truck was trying to tune his radio to hear NPR announce the latest ISIS attack after an afternoon of fishing, hit it. The accident occurred the week of my birthday after not even two years of ownership when I was hell-bent on assimilating and living the "real" Bostonian dream of eating fish and chips "down the Cape" with Michelle. Some people don't notice a loud red Mustang with aftermarket mufflers and speakers blasting indie-rock cruising along, especially if they're daydreaming and sozzled, but the police always did. They routinely pointed their radar gun in my direction. I was accustomed to being escorted to work on a pretty regular basis. That's not because of speeding or other law-breaking pursuits; red cars seem to pique some people's interest as much as a doughnut shop drive-through.

Not that the Lincoln was any better.

It probably didn't help that the white whale hit the streets during the *Reservoir Dogs* era, when everyone became suspicious of the low-riding boat cars. Michelle and I also spent a lot of time shampooing its enormous trunk right when Walter White gave trunks, the Southwest, and automated car washes a particular reputation. By the time we ran out of patience and sticky carpet coins, some fellow car wash enthusiasts were also worried, and we decided that was as clean as the stained carpet could get. After considerable remorse, I felt the same way about the Mustang even after the body shop's extensive repairs and I waxed the swirly hell out of it, still disappointed the car wasn't quite right since being disfigured.

Nice people can't have nice things, and I hope my wife doesn't trade me in just because I'm repaired. I can't buff that scar out. It's more permanent than the tattoo of the Marvel character I fantasize about her getting.

WINTER TIRES ARE MORE than nice. They are a riot. There was one snowstorm where I drove to work in the Mustang as confident as Captain America and headed back home around noon. The ride home became dicey, when I was finally convinced a rally car might be the better choice in coffee milk land, or at least I should've added some cat litter to the trunk for extra weight. The rear axle kept reminding me it was too light, and I briefly wondered if I should've swapped the Lincoln's guardian angel amulet to this car for some much needed protection. There was a tractor-trailer on its side, one or two Jeeps practicing their slow-crawl winter maneuvers that I barreled past, even though there were no visible lanes anymore. The snow was too deep to drive the car. The four winter tires mounted on aftermarket steel wheels ferried me home unscathed, indeed a remarkable feat. However, by the time I plowed into the driveway, I was developing a headache from focusing so hard on *not* dying.

The magical Mustang scraped by the icebergs, with better results than the *Titanic*, fishtailing its way across I-95 like a champ. I'm sure any action hero wouldn't have looked more incredible driving the red coupe. Still, after this white-knuckle joyride, I now understood why so many actors who enjoy cars prefer tending to vineyards in California over winter wonderland drudgery. The winter rally also hinted at why most of the impatient New Englanders drive bro-trucks and SUVs while stoned. The white fluff stresses you after a while. Every snowfall made traveling difficult, and the salt eventually killed anything you drove. I was sick of getting tailed every week by the police and witnessing rust ruining what I enjoyed, so I traded the Mustang without too much remorse.

I needed something stick and all-wheel-drive so winter wouldn't suck so bad and I could be as cool as my wife. My back must've necessitated something more comfortable too, because that basic seat bothered me on long trips. Something was achy and tight in the lumbar region, and I blamed the car. I also didn't want to garnish as much attention as a Hollywood icon anymore with insurance in Massachusetts being overpriced. *Understated* seemed cooler, anyway, despite my earlier fears of boredom.

HOSPITAL IN BOSTON

THE CHAPEL AND THE SHORE

JUNE 2021

THE DOCTOR ASKED me to close my eyes and think of a "nice, relaxing place" where I vacationed as a kid to distract me while he tested my reflexes, so I closed my eyes and reminisced about the Jersey Shore. What a mistake. I should've thought of the relaxing high-altitude desert forests teeming with aspens, cottonwoods, and pinion pines, or a quaint fall hike through the Arboretum in Coconino County with Michelle.

A TYPICAL CHILDHOOD SUMMER

THE OCEAN WAS TRYING TO KILL US, but we visited it every summer anyway. Sharks prowled the waters, oil tar spills and medical waste littered the shore, and rip currents kept me from exploring the water above my waist. I remember hugging the tie-dye boogie board so hard you could see indentions in the foam because my survival depended on it. One particular Jersey shore boardwalk was possessed by a carnival clown convention when I was only 8 or 9, but somehow I survived the experience. Seagulls once stole my peanut butter sandwich and bit my finger. Sunlight gave my shoulders second-degree burns, and we side-stepped the jellyfish minefield that surfaced every August.

If my parents splurged, we would pack ice in a giant cooler, waiting for the wind to pick up to eat salty, sandy hoagies. It was an exercise in futility, facing our backs to the breeze. All the while defending our lunch from hungry seagulls and retreating from crashing sea-foam that was slowly invading our sprawling towel and umbrella bivouac. We hauled our gear and beach furniture around like a gypsy caravan, but the only highlight was the hoagie lunch and bronzed college girls playing beach volleyball nearby. The sport was better watched in person than the Summer Olympics dedicated to the event (before 4K TVs were invented). Is that the only reason I attended college?

California girls like Arizona and beach sports.

Disney popularized pirate lifestyles, so we were suspicious that sort might be lurking in the seaweed that floated by or hiding beneath the boardwalk planks with the homeless people. We were inspired to dig holes in the sand with the tenacity of an Oak Island enterprise until we inevitably hit water. Although I never found gold or any veritable treasure, there was always the boardwalk to lift our spirits. My mom would warn us about everything unsafe in the tide and the characters who visited it: "Don't stand too far out on the pier. It might float away. Use more sun lotion since the sun is burning you. Don't go out so far.

The rip current will drown you. I thought I saw a shark. Pick up that needle or cigarette butt and I'll give *your* hoagie to that homeless guy. Just take a break, and let's walk to the antiques and saltwater taffy shops back on the boardwalk."

Before we could even utter something as inappropriate as "how about the arcade?" additional social commentary vetoed our protests: "Stay away from the tattoo shops where those water-ice girls in bikinis are hanging out." *But maybe Keira Knightley was there,* I wondered. *Oh well, back to the dangerous ocean. Hopefully, sharks don't like hoagies and if they do maybe a volleyball girl will save me if I sink.*

JUNE 2021

I USUALLY AVOID roofs, the ocean, and carnivals because of past traumatic events. I also dread surprises and synthetic cotton-flavored candy with the consistency of brittle hair resembling a clown's colorful wig. Even though the halls weren't lined with down-on-their-luck jesters, the hospital on the day of my surgery was also not very inviting. I knew that, unlike the clowns, the doctor's purpose was to help, but I couldn't help worrying if it would all be in vain. There remained so many unanswered questions and only a partial diagnosis, but the surgery was supposed to address those.

It didn't start off very promising. Enroute to an elevator, I passed the hospital church. I asked the administrative woman in a suit who was ushering me to the following location if that was the only chapel in the building.

"Oh, that's the only one."

I nodded. "Well, I guess that's where my family is ..."

Glancing up from a text from Michelle, I wished I was with them instead of where I was supposed to be going. The text said something about "waiting in the chapel to pray for me."

I was glad because I needed all the prayer I could get.

According to some people and the Good Book, prayer is

powerful and can move mountains. I just wanted to *see* mountains again or eat funnel cake and hoagies with my spouse, preferably in the desert, where observing a distant rainstorm drenching someone else while remaining safe and dry was routine. The rain brought out the distinct smell of the desert plants and soil, and a flash flood was fantastic to watch from a scenic vista or even the fucking Walmart parking lot littered with RVs. In Virginia, the storms ruined *everyone's* day.

The hospital seemed on par, but I was in a foul mood since checking in and probably not the best candidate for judging experiences. I'm sure there is an app for that, and I couldn't care less about giving anyone "stars" or filling out surveys. If I did, though, I think it would be brutally honest and get canceled.

Ten stars for telling me I'm fucking screwed.

Nine stars for saving me before it's too late.

Eight stars for telling me I don't have COVID-19.

Seven stars for spelling my name right and maybe 100 negative stars for shutting down a chapel during the worst time of most people's lives as they trudge toward the operating wing.

My candid response startled the suit lady as the elevator door slammed shut. She looked miserable and perhaps preferred reciting rules over the rosary, or maybe she was sick of scrolling through surveys and negative feedback.

"Say what?" she asked.

"The chapel. My family said they are in the chapel praying for me," I confirmed.

"Oh, well, they *shouldn't* be in there—*no one should be in there! The pandemic, you know, closed it.*"

I gulped, embarrassed, and laughed instead of rattling off all the profanities streaming through my head. "Oh, I guess I shouldn't have said anything. I blew their cover."

The woman in the suit did not look amused, and I wish I had revealed nothing, now fully expecting my three family members to be hauled out of a hospital chapel because they were prayer criminals now. How horrible and ironic yet fitting for the first phase of addressing my sudden diagnosis, which began with a riveting phone call rivaling the childhood clown nightmare. I started praying they would evade detection by hospital security so that they could pray for me to get through the most significant challenge (besides surviving the ocean visits) I was about to face in my entire life. The challenge would begin with a laminectomy and some kind of lumbar drain. After the initial consultation two weeks prior, the neurosurgeon simply suggested, *"Don't Google that."*

VILLAIN NUMBER 4: THE POSER RALLY CAR

DECEMBER 2017

AT FIRST, the clutch wasn't torturous, so I drove everywhere with the white economy poser rally car, especially anywhere all-wheel drive would be helpful. We embarked on a grand East Coast tour from summer 2017 to fall 2018, usually in perilous environments. Destinations included the famous Mount Washington and the infamous Pagoda landmark in Reading, Pennsylvania, an iconic monument that is always lit up red at night and perched on the edge of a steep, twisting road that rally enthusiasts race up each year, probably for pretzels. Reading is where I was born, and since I have family in the area, we try to visit them every year. But long trips were becoming more complex, and the winding roads burned my clutch leg, making me wince with an ever noticeable pain somewhere in my low back around L3. I shrugged it off; with enough stretching and pain pills, I could get by.

However, it is now apparent the villains were getting cocky and more brazen, but I was too distracted trying not to die while driving on unfamiliar hilly terrain. The prospect of picking up some of my favorite culinary treats I had been deprived of since moving to the land of dairy and football seemed to make the pain worth the gain.

I DON'T KNOW the real reason mass-produced snacks are as savory as a bowl of dry cat food. If you have never had an authentic pretzel pulled out of a 100-year-old brick oven by some mulish guy pushing around a wheelbarrow and spewing a coal cough, you don't know what you're missing. "Store pretzels" have been swindling you. I suggest tossing them in the trash, use them as kindling, and head to Pennsylvania. Bribe a bodyguard to hit the streets of specific seedy Reading neighborhoods to pursue a life-changing pretzel quest, and pretend you're Don Quixote but with an unmistakable accent leaning heavily on the "r's." Just say "war-tar" when thirsty and mutter something about traffic on "the Schuylkill Expressway" when people ask where you're from. Maybe the locals won't notice uncontrollable fear and piss-stained pants as you hastily abandon the noble search for pretzel gold mines. Urban "Penn-see" is probably very different from anywhere else. Pick up some "war-tar ice" if you survive the pretzel experience. You'll be glad you did. Pretzels will make you thirsty and craving something as sweet as a shoofly pie.

The state is in decline with American manufacturing, the coal is dirty now, and a controversial gas pipeline fucked up the fields, scenery, and morale. Thanks to communism, the internet, and same-day delivery, China cranks out everything cheaper. Besides, property taxes in the Keystone State are not budget-minded, so the local economies can be as morose as an unsalted, cold pretzel. The last time I visited family in the area, you still had to go in person to get a proper Philly cheesesteak or hoagie. Technology doesn't always catch up to some places as quickly and some businesses are stubbornly old-school.

You may be familiar with Reading because of the pretzels it

cranks out of a few well-known factories and even fewer lesser-known crumbling holes in the walls that are getting harder to find. They are usually inconspicuous, hidden between dilapidated row houses infested with criminals and crack whores or semiabandoned warehouses that folded up when international competition or domestic tax laws burned them. Seriously, though, that is where the best pretzel establishments are. The sawdusty, hollow dry shit you've been buying in the grocery store is just the leftover debris they sweep off the floor. *Those* pretzels are as cheap as an Amish tax bill and as tasteless as an apple dumpling without the apples.

If you're from the Lancaster area or near Reading, you know the best pretzels are in the unmarked bags, but I don't blame outsiders for being apprehensive. It's the same as buying weed in the state-run store or licensed establishment versus the potent product you purchase from the guy with face tattoos driving around in a tinted Chrysler 300. Sometimes, a little risk goes a long way. If you're afraid to take risks you shouldn't be wandering around Reading, searching for pretzels, or mistaking the face tattoo guy for someone you're supposed to meet from Christian Mingle. Go to the mall and settle for culinary mediocrity; it's much safer.

OUR ENTOURAGE ARRIVED in convoy mode, behind a white Mustang that my brother drove because my previous choice of vehicles must've inspired him. *Maybe I am an excellent influence?* I was relieved to find parking on the street because parking spaces were scarce and low-profile sport tires scare the shit out of some drivers attempting to parallel park. I almost missed the disguised pretzel building.

"You think it's safe, EJ?" I asked after locking the car, glancing over at a younger version of myself.

"Sure, I guess," he replied.

The answer was bullshit, and we both knew it. EJ lit a

cigarette to calm his nerves as muffled voices at the end of the block caught our attention. We quickly crossed the street. We had a good reason to be where we shouldn't have been. The lure of the pretzels was calling, and the hidden door to the establishment swung open in time for us to catch a whiff of the oven cranking out golden brown piping-hot deliciousness by a stressed-out German lady. I suspected business was booming, but I didn't know or even care. I just wanted the goods before getting mugged, shot, or before the shifty-eyed guy with a wheelbarrow threw *us* into the oven because the kindling pile looked kind of low.

Some rich snob and a snobby kid who may have been his grandson dashed out with a sack of steaming loot in a brown paper bag. The duo jumped into an idling Range Rover, and the six-figure SUV sped off down a narrow one-way alley. This was definitely the right place. I checked my pocket for the cash, giving the parked cars one last look, hoping they would still be there when we returned. Reservations aside, it was time to time travel, pick up some pretzel loot, and rally to the top of the hill with some family for a "relaxing adventure."

If there's one thing I've learned over the years, it is that "family" and "relaxing adventure" are always mutually exclusive.

We were not in a race to reach the top of the road leading to the Pagoda, but I was as nervous as a student pilot on a solo flight with a broken radio and a sputtering engine. I was sweating while Michelle leaned against the window turning green, listening to my backseat codriver mom providing encouraging shifting tips (she was more experienced in uphill enthusiast driving). Select the wrong gear at a hairpin turn on an unfamiliar rain-drenched road when driving stick shift in an underpowered car, and language can become explicit. I didn't want us all to die, and I never forgot that one incident in Virginia when I power-slided into boulders, so the cursing continued until we reached the top.

I may have bummed a cigarette from my brother at the top of

the summit to overwhelm the burning clutch smell trapped in my nostrils, and it was at that specific moment the car's under-powered engine was as obvious as a mustard-stained sleeve. Eventually, I would loathe the clutch. It was causing pain to shoot up my leg, but that pain wasn't fully realized until I traded up to the adequately powered rally car my heart was set on buying.

INTERMISSION I: THE CEDAR TREE

THE EXACT DAY or month of the "tree rescue" in Michelle's family's backyard remains as unclear as our future. The time frame is vague, escaping our sharp memories with the same bittersweet, ambivalent haze that seems to define our past.

We are pretty confident it was somewhere around 2017 when we plucked the sad sapling from the ground, transferring it to a pot. When two or three inches tall, Michelle rescued the suspected cedar tree because the shade of a towering row of established hemlocks was choking it. The pot wasn't huge, but the feeble tree was happy to be moved to a sunny spot with an excellent plot of land all to its own.

I was jealous.

Michelle placed the pot where it was visible every time you went in and out of the house, and it seemed to provide us with an unspoken pledge that by the time it outgrew the pot, we better be living in a place of our own, credit scores, debt-to-income ratios, 20 percent down payments, and emergency funds notwithstanding.

VILLAIN NUMBER 5: THE SNOWMOBILE

FEBRUARY 2018

IT WAS WINTER, and we were ready for a snowmobiling adventure in Maine. My wife and I desperately needed an intermission from a stonewalled reality that was a scintilla better than "the Beltway swamp" but nowhere as soul-stirring as Arizona and the time we reminisced about before student loans. We were nearing the end of our terrible 20s, sinking like a heavy coal barge plagued with villains addicted to drilling holes in the hull. It seemed like we were not much better off than our Boston restart, despite all the overtime hours, frugality, and positive thinking. The only glimmer of hope kicking off the year was my disguised glee at the recent Super Bowl LII upset of the New England Patriots by my hometown heroes, the Philadelphia Eagles (which left everyone else depressed).

I was tempted to shimmy up a light post to celebrate the underdog kicking the establishment in their perfect bleached teeth, but New England is a kind of dark place with too many rules, and that stunt would've been embarrassing. Besides, I never cared about sports much except for hockey, and seeing everyone else bitter only lifted my spirits as briefly as the president's plan was trending to form a military parade "like they did in France." *Maybe only the aliens that Tom DeLonge had been chosen to warn us about would understand that plan, politics be damned as flying reptilian Tic Tac bastards fucking with our already fragile world.*

What we really needed was an extended vacation to relax and recover from our "outside jobs" and the three years of mediocre progress torching the towering debt that was delaying our independence and crushing our esprit de corps. I doubt a parade would have changed decades of economic and political irresponsibility; it probably was as helpful as expecting a vacation to solve our problems. Still, we should've canceled the vacationing adventure, run away, joined the Quebec Winter Carnival, and dodged educational loans like some people dodged the draft back in the '70s, Canadian style.

That would've been one hell of a way to restart.

THE SNOWMOBILING idea initially sounded like an excellent recovery plan. It wasn't the first time we had experienced the "north country" or the "sleds," as enthusiasts referred to them. I now had a few years of New Englander life experience under my snow pants, jeans, sweatpants, long underwear, and belt, so I *thought* I knew what to expect. I was practically an expert at recovering from hurting myself when the ferocious winter months hit, turning the walkways into polished glass and my bottom a particular shade of bruised plum. Of course, Michelle was a native, so it was more of a reunion than an adventure for her. Not being a novice on a machine that propels to triple-digit speeds on a literal ice sheet is a good thing. There is not much room for error should something go wrong in adverse conditions, especially since we were far from any reputable hospitals.

We were in convoy mode (a recurring life feature, it seems) with my wife, her family, and some friends. My father-in-law was the "trail boss," and he took the role seriously. Equipped with the fastest and loudest snow-propelling machine, he tore through the trails like a veteran rider, loving absolutely everything about the sport. The preparation was perhaps as necessary as the actual event, and his stable of fine breeds were meticulously "tuned up" for every snow adventure weekend that could be squeezed out of the short winter months. If he could have his way, there would be a snowmobile displayed in the living room year-round as proudly as some people flaunt a Steinway baby grand. The dictionary defines "trail boss" as a person responsible for driving a herd of cattle, so I guess my father-in-law, whom I call "Mr. C," was an Italian version of John Wayne, and I'm as cool as the Fonz.

Perhaps I was living in a spaghetti Western, or so it seemed.

Every great actor requires an excellent supporting cast, and every snowmobile vacation needs a backup trail boss. My brother-in-law filled the role. He rode an identical machine, a '90s vintage sled with exhaust modifications, and since he was the tallest was also the most qualified to colead our expedition. The rest of the cattle weren't decked out as luxuriously as the higher echelons, which meant rented machines with less control and reduced speed.

The weather was getting progressively shittier, and the trail-grooming crew was overworked or preoccupied, maybe dreaming of the weather in Florida. The undergroomed trails left a lot to be desired. Of course, they were very crowded, and to be honest, less experienced members of our group were performing some dangerous stunts. We were lucky no one wound up killed or injured. I think it's safe to assume the competent, and amateur, members were experiencing similar misery and fatigue. The trail boss even experienced migraine-induced vomiting. The sleet pelted my icy visor, and my breath was clouding it—just further subterfuge at any prospect of clear vision.

I cursed inside my helmet a salvo of colorful adult obscenities, matching the cadence of a paintball gun and the artistic complexity of a 1996 Mystic Cobra, and I wouldn't dare utter any of that in the presence of my mother-in-law. She was riding at the back of our escort. I could've used a volley of adult beverages to numb the stupidity. Still, I was responsible, polite, and stuck to my lukewarm coffee-filled thermos stained red by tomato soup.

The unpleasant trip turned sour. I assumed it was a bust because of colliding environmental and personality factors, leading to a medley of remarkable off-trail "incidents" committed by a young, resilient redheaded girl who wasn't sure what turning, slowing, or stopping meant. In a separate instance, foggy prescription eyeglasses prevented another group member from seeing the trail and eventually riding the machine. To be successful in this sport, vision is critical. However, an inclination to competitiveness among certain members seemed to fuel the most compelling haphazardness, resulting in irreversible damage.

At least everyone was wearing a high-quality helmet.

These unexpected intermissions and the cannonball-run drama more than annoyed Michelle and I, so we chose our own break. It seemed like a reasonable idea, but then again, we have little loyalty to group events. We pulled off the trail at one point, shut the engines down, waddled over in our sweat-soaked layers to a safer place, and took in the beautiful views. I can appreciate the Appalachians in the Northeast and can tolerate the frigid, brutal New England temperatures, but they were not as soothing as the grandeur of the Southwest. It was reminding me of being confined to antenna TV programming after years of premium cable, because student loans can cause those kinds of compromises, as well as sweet V-Twin motorcycle purchases being delayed.

Steaming in the knee-high snow, we snapped a few pictures, regained our composure, fantasized about stringing Christmas lights on cactuses in 75-degree weather, and took a coffee break. Coffee is always relaxing, even in a crisis. Likewise, the desert is always comforting, even when it snows.

If the experience has evaded your life, you haven't lived. Watch a Boho camper van desert-themed glamping video, order some Taco Bell from an app, and pop a CBD gummy bear in your mouth like a real 21st-century badass.

THE SIESTA WAS SHORT-LIVED, as the sound of a returning scout from our group echoed in the distance. Perplexed to see our enjoyment at *not* snowmobiling, he quickly informed us that the trail boss and Nitro Circus did not realize where we were and that stopping unannounced violated "trail code." Apparently, our recklessness meant we were in more trouble than a disgruntled ant trying to crawl out of Meteor Crater. Not that we cared. Cancel the snow adventure, and we might actually live long enough to one day hit up "early bird special" buffets and reside in Sun City. The possibility of banishment from the arctic chapter of Hells Angels even sounded durable. If I had received a cell signal in the remote depths of miserable Maine, I would've fired off a red-eye flight search for Yuma or even Sin City. In fact, banish me to fucking Iceland for all I care—I'd probably thrive with all the yogurt and less brutal winters than what we were experiencing in full force.

We could run away to the remote Nordic island, become dual citizens, live in a frugal homemade igloo as part-time hackers. Take full advantage of the Icelandic Student Loan Fund, and return to our homeland seven years later with a few PhDs to brag about. The plan sounds complicated and as speculative as Assange's fate. I'm not sure if working for WikiLeaks is excellent on a résumé or perhaps a treason bullet.

Michelle and I prefer to enjoy a few moments alive then hours spent hauling hundreds of pounds out of deep snow because some people don't learn their limits or drink discolored thermos coffee. This may have been the breaking point in our Maine adventure. The tension was as incredible as the few minutes leading up to a street hockey dispute when I was a kid, but, really, it probably marked what most people have experienced during dysfunctional family vacations: a mental countdown to its conclusion.

I would have preferred to hug a saguaro in my birthday suit than push forward, but I'm not usually a poor sport. Now, I wish I was a poor sport. It would have spared me some pain.

AFTER FIVE HOURS of traveling in frigid temperatures, the vacation turned snafu began before we even arrived at the cabin. We took a photo of the car's thermometer halfway to the destination because a minus sign in front of the number was comical. It should have caused us to turn around, but as firstborns we rarely quit anything we started because of guilt and work ethic. The trip north was also the first winter-themed rally in the poser rally car that's only saving grace was its five-speed and all-wheel-drive. So, the trip had *that* going for it: an excellent, newer, reasonable vehicle replacing the Mustang that cost less than what some people spend on snowmobiles that don't even have cupholders. Even though it wasn't the cool rally car that I honestly wanted, I convinced myself that Suze Orman's advice was somehow sexy.

"Wow, this thing hugs the road and grips like glue!" I patted the dashboard once between a perfectly timed rev match.

"Yeah, *great*." Michelle looked sick.

"We will carve up these ice-covered, avalanche-prone mountain roads and show those stupid trucks how much money they wasted!" I bragged. I downshifted the coarse, underpowered engine every chance I could to feel as drifty as Ken Block.

"Another doughnut, please," I asked my companion codriver every few miles between sips of iced coffee, reminding her of power-to-weight ratios and automobile suspension configurations.

Drivers had to stay alert up north to avoid the occasional ice sheets flying off tractor-trailer roofs. Whenever we headed to Maine, our routine pit stop was at Tim Hortons because nitro-style coffee beverages increase alertness, and sometimes you need that kind of motivation when traveling through a frozen hell. Preparing for the tundra often made us reconsider our packing choices before reaching the "Vacationland" state. Did I bring enough thermal underwear? Boots? Scarves and 50 pairs of socks? Sweatpants to wear *between* the jeans and the thermal underwear? *Who the hell enjoyed this kind of voluntary frigidness?*

But then again, I was voluntarily chugging iced coffee in the winter and eating doughnut balls pervertedly named after some guy named Tim, which also made little sense.

Popping more doughnuts from the Canadian dozen—which is 10 because counting with mittens is difficult when it's that cold—somehow motivated us to continue our expedition. After driving for a few hours, ascending the steep mountain, we pulled up to the snow-covered campsite. The circus had packed up its tent and moved to a different town, but since family is as essential as toothpaste, they compelled us to join the procession, even to the far ends of civilization. I swore that "the greatest show on Earth" had been canceled the previous summer, causing the carnies to take new job offers in Washington or return to Eastern Europe.

Guess I was wrong.

THE TERRAIN in rural Maine is always reliably magnificent. Tall snow-crested trees surrounded the trails, distant peaks and nearby bridges passing over icy waterfalls provided a backdrop as quaint as any Bob Ross painting, and the frozen lakes suggested the Earth *was* flat.

Huh, maybe that old Arizona guy warning people in the Fry's parking lot was right! I assumed he only ever lived in a flat parking lot.

Now I'm not sure. Perhaps he was an ice angler from Maine who was banned from sharing local geography. Some people just have that kind of bad luck.

They should ban some people from taking vacations. Still, they're probably the same people pushing "cancel culture" agendas schemed up while "tech detox" vacationing, so they are untouchable. Endless natural beauty is hard to ignore, but as the day progressed, chaotic charades again interrupted the admirable geography, and denylisting seemed as reasonable as being politically incorrect. We turned around a sharp turn to witness another "off-trail" episode featuring an upside-down "snowblower" with a member of our group predictably waving for help. This time we had to flip the tunneling snow machine around, and at least three of us had to drag and push the damn thing to get it back to something resembling a trail. The "trail boss" may have dislocated a hip, shoulder, or both, and I feared this would be his rendition of Shackleton's fourth expedition. He vomited and returned to the cabin to recover from the ordeal.

Our sad group continued anyway, somehow agreeing we didn't want to waste the day and still had lunch to look forward to at a restaurant. *If we make it there alive,* I pondered, wishing for a veto to yet another questionable call by "trail boss" management and yearning for something to eat that didn't have beans in it. Our contribution to the vacation was good humor and positivity, and eating the leftover food we brought because it wasn't popular. Michelle made chili, transported it to Maine in a bag, and was dumbfounded that no one else thought a thawed double-bagged gallon of chili looked appetizing.

Like poor management and unsightly bagged chili, I had experienced "signaling" before, which is when you hold up one hand and varying fingers to let oncoming riders know how many riders remained in your party. This time, it was a mistake. I was approaching a slight dip in the trail, bobbed my head, raised my left hand, lost control, tried to counter it with a quick pull to the left, and veered off course in a twisted sideways maneuver that somehow missed any large trees. I briefly closed my eyes, convinced I was a dead man.

Probably paralyzed, I remember worrying, *or something at the very least must have broken. I hate the snow, and I hate this ridiculous sport. The landscape is killer, but not worth it if the redheaded girl or this lawn mower with skis and a pathetic excuse of a windshield kills me.*

Seconds that seemed longer than minutes passed.

I stood up. Everything ached, something pinched in my back, and my hip felt stabbed. The rest of our unhappy ensemble heard I had an accident and returned to help haul the machine back onto the trail, relieved I seemed to be intact. Everyone had a lot of search-and-rescue practice throughout the day, so by the time it was my turn to replicate a cringeworthy accident, no one was phased. It seemed miraculous, though, that I wasn't bleeding or impaled. I was just grateful my bones weren't visible and that we didn't wind up on an episode of *North Woods Law.* The accident shattered nothing except my dwindling confidence, and I never gripped the handles as tightly as I did after that.

Convinced my guardian angel was still on the job (although maybe a little lethargic), I was relieved to have avoided such a close call with a potentially fatal outcome. I half-stood and half-sat on the barely noticeable heated seat for the rest of the journey. There was an unshakeable pain that was bothersome and uncomfortable. At that moment I vowed I hated the sport of the lawnmower-skis and wanted nothing to do with it ever again. I never returned to take part in another *Evel Knievel on Ice!* tribute, qualifying this accident as the most apparent villain to wreak havoc on my delicate disks.

HOSPITAL IN BOSTON

ANGELS AND THE WALKER SCAM

JUNE 2021

THE EVENTS that transpired over the few weeks preceding my hospital adventure landed me in the realm of some Hitch-cock-style horror movie shitshow, helpless and dazed. I wouldn't be surprised if they billed the coffee tab to the insurance company during my distressing state, but I doubted that would be legal. The nurses were incredible angels on Earth, handing me the cold or hot coffee they had brewed every morning before the cafeteria opened. It seemed like the only nice thing to happen during a terrible time. However, the physical therapists had me sign some convoluted contract, and I'm no lawyer. I was loopy as fuck and battling a caffeine-withdrawal headache, nodding my head and agreeing to the walker spiel. Unfortunately, I don't think they brewed something as bold as what I'm used to, which affected my focus, but they seemed to push walkers on everyone they could. It wasn't just me. They must work on commission or something. The sight of a walker instantly reminds me of an old-person home, which conjures up some unsettling trigger words like *hospice*, *fiber*, *decaf*, and *death*. I'd bet a sawbuck or two they line the road to hell with the two-wheeled contraptions. I don't want to find out and don't have any cash to spare.

All I know for a fact is insurance doesn't cover the wretched thing.

It's thrown in the back of a closet now, with the tag still on it, hiding behind boxes of Christmas ornaments because looking at it reminds me of the hospital, and vexing about a future being paralyzed or dead.

I DON'T KNOW if a magnificent rainbow has gold at the end of it or a portal to hell, but the last time I remember seeing one, I was being ripped off in a New Hampshire coffee shop with an unpleasant taste in music. They prefer the self-serve approach in the towns we visit around the White Mountains, yet charge more than Dunkin', make you do most of the work, and boldly ask on the credit card screen, "Would you like to add a tip?" *No, not really.* I have to save my extra money to buy necessities like food and walkers and, if I inherit gold one day, to pay for all the taxes that might incur.

The local grocery stores often request contributing a dollar or two to cancer causes, which we used to ignore just like the cereals in the aisle run by the Big Sugar cartel. Michelle recently announced she now presses "yes" in light of life-changing events. Of course, I'm not opposed to that because I'm sure someone is being helped after administration fees. I don't even care about the money, since I never had much to begin with, and sometimes it can't solve a health crisis. But maybe if I bequeath enough, they'll hand the coffee to me one day when I pay for it, as they did in Boston when I could barely sit up on the hospital bed. That would be nice.

VILLAIN NUMBER 6: THE REAL RALLY CAR

DECEMBER 2018

THE CAR SALES associate warned me before I bought the honest-to-god rally car with a cult following and substantial street credibility, and Michelle was a witness: "Don't buy that specific model unless you want to visit the chiropractor, bro."

OK, sure. But I'm young and have a history with cool cars. I walk every day to perform my job, so I'll be fine. You must be old, like 40 or something, and jealous. Probably drive some economy shitbox, you're just frugal, or your hero kids are 20 and still living in the basement mining crypto and spiking the electric bill. Not my problem, bro.

It wasn't more than a year and some change later when I ignored the sales associate's advice, pulled the trigger, and traded the poser rally car for something extraordinary. It was one of those purchases that shouldn't have happened, and I instantly regretted it.

The first sign to "run away" was when I slammed my index finger in the driver's side door after a quick test drive, provoking the alarmed sales associate to run us back to where the mechanics deal with medical mishaps. He handed me a few feet of gauze and a roll of tape, remarking that if I didn't want to go to the hospital, maybe I should be brave and just buy the car since we were blood brothers now. I agreed, signing away the very persecutory purchasing agreement with a throbbing hand. The acquisition even violated my car-buying code: I bought an extended service contract.

"Rally cars are complicated and fragile," warned the finance expert.

Luckily, I canceled the scam a few weeks later for a prorated refund. I'm not a total fool, I think.

I THOUGHT I needed a stick-shift car with rally pedigree because Michelle drove only third-pedal vehicles, and my entire childhood was influenced by the immortal *Fast and Furious* franchise. Admittedly, though, I was bored with cars quicker than was financially prudent, foolishly trading them around like those guys in all the automotive-themed reality TV shows.

The poser rally car was slow by my ever-increasing high-speed standards, and if I had been racing it on an old convex TV back in my video game heyday, I would have upgraded it with a turbo. Besides, yearning for those fun times when I was young and daring, I would reminisce about the memorable experiences in the Lincoln, which we had retired to a barn since it was constantly experiencing mechanical failures. The barn even caught fire at one point, but the cursed luxury coupe escaped with mere cosmetic scarring. Undrivable, unrepairable, unsellable, dangerous, but incapable of departing this Earth: quite a legacy, and I'm not surprised since, you know, it's cursed.

THE REAL RALLY car should've turned a new page in our long-standing road trip saga, but it mostly sat in a dirt area on the side of the driveway I cleverly dubbed "the rally lot." After making a few local trips, my leg was always irritated, and something pinched in my low back. I blamed the heavy clutch action, the too-tight suspension, the uncomfortable seats with lack of lumbar support. Perhaps I shouldn't have trashed the Brit pop CD the previous owner left in the player. Hell, it may have been as critical as the cross in the cellar you don't remove from the creepy haunted house.

I bet it was that awful CD.

The car needed it, like how the weird-sounding, disgruntled Volkswagen bug needed a female companion in the late '90s. *I should have upgraded to anything above the base model or bought something luxurious. Perhaps a newer Lincoln, like Matthew McConaughey.*

I blamed practically anything else about the rigid, rally torture box and its interaction with the potholed Massachusetts roads that made driving as intolerable as barreling over a series of frost heaves with tireless rims. It was a terrible relationship, and, like many of those, it was abusive and needed to end. After months of threatening its fate with a sore, crooked finger and achy back, I demanded an immediate automotive divorce. Until now, I had never taken a pain pill in my life, except for the rare misguided occasion I quit coffee and experienced the wrath of a caffeine-withdrawal headache. Sometimes you need to restart certain habits and traditions, and occasionally I was convinced that coffee addictions are as harmful as drugs.

Not a belief I hold anymore, though. Some addictions are as helpful to some people as scams, and purchasing too many cars in one's lifetime might classify as an addiction. I might have a real fucking problem now that I think about it; the rally car was no more of a Herbie than I was a stunt car driver.

After two months of lamentable rally car ownership, by the time spring had arrived, I was sitting in a chiropractor's office, barely able to walk, popping ibuprofen with the casualness of popcorn. This was a low moment, and I was exhausted from contemplating how that car could be more cursed than the Lincoln that it sent me to seek professional medical attention. It also sent me to sleep on the floor. Because maybe the curse wasn't confined to the car—perhaps it was the mattress?

OVER A DECADE OF PRACTICING, Michelle and I developed elaborate methods for flipping and spinning various mattresses around, reminiscent of a juggling circus act. We couldn't figure out why they always seemed to interrupt our sleep and create that achy uncomfortableness. I should clarify that by "we," I mean "I." Michelle could sleep on the floor, or a board, or rocks, or *anything*, as she often claimed during the rotating mattress exercise we practiced at least semiannually. I remember one frustrating rotation ritual when I suggested a revised quarterly plan. Clearly, the problem seemed to be me. I was too picky, too accustomed to I'm not sure what, but perhaps my expectations for comfort were vain, unrealistic, and *rich*. We often debated whether my tastes were too upscale for sleeping comfort, as we left a trail of mattress from Virginia to New England.

The first was the traditional spring. That lasted only a year.

The second was the foam-in-a-box mattress. Maybe two years.

The third was an expensive foam delivered by mattress professionals.

The fourth was a borrowed spare, handcrafted by local artisans (desperation was setting in).

The fifth returned to the third since handcrafted by local artisans doesn't mean better.

The sixth was "trying out the floor" because India may have been trending.

The seventh was a "hybrid: in a box." I now am convinced a "hybrid" is a clever scam disguising the "worst of both worlds."

The eighth was the most extravagant, a traditional spring with foam and other complicated layers. It was also the heaviest and most durable, and sold with a ridiculous warranty that may expire when our mortgage does.

I think that was it. The ninth may signal divorce, and I'll potentially be intentionally kicked to the street, homeless, and have to sleep on cardboard pizza boxes (which I have never tried yet). All the mattresses and methods did not last very long, except for the final one, which we still have because soon after that purchase, I recognized the problem was *not* the product. It was the *user*. Besides, it may have another 20 years of factory-backed guarantee, so we have to keep it forever, or at least until the housing market cools, which might be the same time.

Rolling out of bed, I continued to curse whatever current cheap piece of crap we were sleeping on, figuring achy backs turned unsuspecting young people into villains by 30 and if the right one came along, my fate might be different. The ideal mattress never came along, so I decided the "right" one remained as elusive as the Lost Dutchman's Gold Mine in Arizona, and the many "bad" mattresses were the actual source of my increasing discomfort.

THE OFFICIAL DIAGNOSIS suggested sacroiliac joints, inflammation, sciatica, some sore muscles, or tendonitis. The doctor of realignment wasn't sure of the cause, but he quickly prescribed a remedy: Just submit to a few cracks, pops, and a scheduled maintenance plan. He suggested repetition was the culprit and that I definitely shouldn't be sleeping on the floor if we owned a mattress. The word *repetition* sounded villainous and evil, so I hated it as much as memory foam mattresses and sport bucket seats. After all, I delivered the mail always looking to the right, holding everything with my left arm, and the human body can get out of alignment, similar to a sensitive rally car. The sales pitch sounded eerily familiar. It made some sense at first, probably because I was in significant pain and couldn't think clearly.

The chiropractor visits, however, became very repetitious, and I suspected a con.

Crack the disks.

Pop the sacroiliac joint.

Stretch the tight hamstring.

Try to avoid crying.

Pay the copay.

Initially, the results seemed promising, so I dropped the maintenance plan as quickly as a western banded gecko discards a tail, convinced I could take care of my issues like I've done with all my vehicles. No one wants to waste money on unnecessary maintenance, mainly because extended service contracts are a scam pushed by "stealerships." I subscribed to the car blogs—I wasn't stupid. Besides, I felt much better after a few sessions and deemed the doctor unnecessary. I could stretch on my own, minus handing over the insurance and credit card twice a week.

Only old, sick, and less active people require routine medical visits. I'm still youthful, healthy, driving stick. Definitely not in that other category.

The chiropractor also gave me what seemed like reasonable, albeit aggravating, advice, which I followed for two more years: "Walking is good for your back."

It was not the first or last time I was told to "walk it off," and the internet seems to support the notion with significant popularity. I'm sure the shoe companies, yoga pants cults, and pedometer app developers are funding these statistics. Conspiracies aside, when returning to work after a week on sick leave or sitting on a plane to elope to the Arizonian desert to marry Michelle, I had to pop a few pain pills despite the time spent resting. It didn't matter if I was in a car, couch, chair, or anywhere else Dr. Seuss would suggest—my back always reminded me that *something* still hurt. Walking at work, while on vacation, or around our block didn't seem to solve the issue; in fact, it frustratingly magnified my symptoms.

I added up the copays and figured I didn't need a walking

coach. I power-walked daily for a living delivering mail to people who didn't want any tree-murdering correspondence and sprinting from dogs who *really* wanted mail or at least a part of my leg. Both activities were performed with no life coaching or step-counting app oversight.

Every time I stepped out of the car I would grimace, loathing the acquisition, especially snarky car sales associates whose predictions were accurate and whose "blood brother" advice was ill-advised. It took me over a year to part ways with the cursed rally car as I yet again shook off another villain playing sinister tricks with my spine.

HOSPITAL IN BOSTON

THE ROOMATE SEQUEL

JUNE 2021

PERSPECTIVE MIGHT CUT DEEPER than the ravines around Glen Canyon Dam, but only when you've experienced it for yourself does the concept hit home. Suppose I was a distressed college dropout living with my parents instead of a hospital patient on the verge of a breakdown disguised as an epiphany. I'd probably educate everyone on perspectives and dedicate a financially lucrative blog or vlog to showcase my experiences. But I'm really not that qualified. I'm a simple car and coffee-loving victim that many elusive villainous entities enjoy harassing. Even the doctors can't figure out why.

The patient next to me (my new hospital roommate) was reminded of "perspective" when asked to put his oxygen back on, even though he believed it was optional.

Perhaps his perspective was delusional.

The oxygen-low alarm wailed incessantly since he arrived, escalating the tension in the room, increasing my already soaring anxiety to record highs. My blood pressure, however, remained predictably low.

It's nothing urgent. He probably just wants attention, or maybe this guy's not a mammal and doesn't need air to breathe.

I was reaching desperation, trying to drown out the noise with the special noise-canceling headphones Michelle had bought me that were not "canceling" enough.

His diagnosis sounded bleak, or at least less promising than mine. It was terrible, but not as rare. I am undoubtedly winning the rarity race, and I honestly don't know the prize.

The nurse continued to refuse his desperate requests to "go outside for fresh air and a cigarette" and, after a volley of complaints, ignored the idiot. She turned her attention to me with a smile, politely leaning over the bed with a flashlight to check the current cerebral fluid level with the casualness that Michelle checks a pizza in the oven. Yet another reminder that perspective was never more apparent, and suddenly everything in our town library's horror section seemed less scary than what I was experiencing in real life. This constant reminder prompted me to figure out how I could have avoided such a fate.

What were the signs I ignored? Who, exactly, were the villains?

Oxygen machines, intravenous lines, and hand sanitizer dispensers buzz, hiss, and emit nuanced tones forming an eerie orchestra when played in unison and on a loop for an entire night. The steady drone of other equipment hums and beeps, repeating an insomniac trance with no sign of stopping—until the human element interrupts it all unexpectedly. The intermission is only for a moment, though, a short-lived reprieve sounding as unequivocally unpleasant as its mechanical counterpart.

The human element proved the most disgusting and maddening, much worse than the physical pain I endured in the ICU. If there's one thing I've learned during the hospital hiatus, roommates are counterproductive to recovery. The most common post-surgery event seems to be when an irritated bedside hand fumbles and claws at the remote control/medical emergency pager, summoning some vague, distressing plea for help. "I need a blanket or flat ice chips or a piss pot emptied or another happy pill if I'm not allowed a cigarette" was the standard line from my neighbor. Still, all there was to distract me from the grating soundtrack was a *Dateline* marathon on maximum volume and the fresh ache of a surgeon's knife in my back, dulled by pediatric-strength pain pills and a robust steroid regimen.

At least the rotating team of attractive nurses was administering them.

I clutched the panic remote every night since arriving, contemplating the surreality of my surroundings and undesirable predicament. The ebb and flow of pain returned with such fervor that only a recipe doctored up in hell could be the origin of such misery.

At least the nurses offered coffee with ice and a straw. I doubt hell is as accommodating, and I don't want to find out.

Night one of my hospital adventure takes the title for "the worst night of my life." Of course, it's no sane person's idea of a good night, but who finds themself at 30 listening to a possible death sentence relayed over the phone? If I had a little more foresight, I would have researched "hospital extended visits" on the internet forums and showed up more prepared. But if *that* internet search didn't have me canceling the entire operation, at least I could've bought some expensive headphones and drowned out the eerie medical symphony with some superior Modest Mouse.

VILLAIN NUMBER 7: THE SUSPICIOUS COOKIE

SOMETIME IN SPRING 2019

IF I COULD TIME TRAVEL, I would have eaten the cookie sooner. I delivered the mail on my assigned route with the typical gusto that would make all postal managers proud. However, I had become accustomed to a certain amount of pain, and I thought I could just "walk off" the problems. This strategy didn't seem to work. The first few months of 2019 marked the first time I encountered a lingering stabbing sensation that would get worse no matter what advice I followed from colleagues, family, and even sporadic urgent care visits. It was as brutal as being pricked by a few hundred Arizona thistles all at once, yet I somehow convinced myself that I could get through it based on little prior pain experience.

Limping my way through most of the day, a compassionate customer (as we called anyone with a mailbox) with a pronounced mistrust of doctors insisted I stop the dangerous ibuprofen regimen and try something *safer* for my stomach. I agreed. Stomach acid was not supposed to be healthy long-term, and I had been popping pain pills like breath mints nonstop for

two months. I was desperate for relief. Against my better judgment, I devoured the suspicious still-warm skunk-tinged baked
good, not caring about precautions such as "good food hygiene."

In my defense, the bastard cookie guy conned me. I honestly
didn't know it was "special," probably because I disregarded
some hurried "time-lapse warning." I was such a good kid my
whole life that I had never experimented with drugs or illegal
substances, even avoiding gum with actual sugar and
discarding pixie sticks at Halloween as if they were cocaine
samplers. My mom may have convinced me they were. And I
guess the electrified, paralyzing pain tingling somewhere
elusively in my low back messed with my decision-making
abilities.

Unsurprisingly, the future rapidly and suspiciously
improved. Specifically, 42 minutes later.

I remember staring at the clock on my phone, wondering
how the hell time started slowing down. Out of nowhere, the
sun became brighter, the mail lighter, and my gait seemed to
improve. I was moving faster, everything seemed more transpar-
ent, and the smell of curry at the apartment complex that usually
burned my nostrils didn't appear so nefarious. Floating from one
building to another, the realization occurred to me that, for the
first moment in two months, *I felt pretty damn good.* It was as
good as back in my desert tenure days before the villains fucked
with my world.

But that's about as long as the good feeling lasted.

Oh, no, I think my spine snapped! The magical answer to why I
was experiencing this fantastic pain-free intermission was
terrifying.

I methodically counted my paces, heading back to the truck,
mentally reviewing my strange condition. The invisible escalator
underneath my feet was somehow propelling my body forward,
effortlessly, so I had plenty of time to think.

*Yep, nothing hurts. The limp is gone. I feel so light I must've lost
some weight in the last half-hour, which explains why I'm thirsty and*

craving a snack and—oh shit! Maybe that cookie was more than just a regular cookie?

I suddenly stopped mid-stride, amused and confounded at my bizarre predicament: Pain pills and turmeric and stretching don't do shit, and if indeed my spine had dislocated itself from my body but still let me walk, I was probably dead or incredibly stoned. In either case, I was royally screwed.

Paranoia-driven adrenaline overwhelmed my system. I was a victim of "thought loops," as they are called, and my sunglasses didn't seem to be tinted dark enough. The world around me spun. Somehow, I drank enough of the blue and glowing "electrolytes-infused" beverage a lovely old lady gave me on my route and splashed enough water on my face in the doughnut shop bathroom to regain an orderly composure. The sunglasses stayed on, though, because the light from the sun was melting my eyes. It was as unpleasant as watching a 3D movie without the complementary blue and red lenses.

I RETURNED to the post office and dragged any remaining mail onto the loading dock. Reluctantly, I entered the building. With a restrained gusto and pale red face, I swung the doors open as if I was The Duke entering a saloon on the set of Old Tucson Studios. Approaching the supervisors with one hand on my head, I explained my perplexing situation. "I'm not feeling well. Maybe I'm dehydrated?" I removed the sunglasses because inside the building it wasn't as bright as the Petrified National Forest anymore and I didn't want to appear to be hiding behind anything suspicious. I definitely had an acute case of red eye, and I was worried my deteriorating condition was as divulging as a junkie's pupils on the *Cowboy Bebop* anime TV series.

After the managers expressed their concern at my peaked appearance, I clocked out and followed their suggestion to retire to the postal basement, where I sprawled out on the couch. Allegedly, it was as haunted as Room 426 of the Hassayampa Inn in Prescott, Arizona, down there, but I didn't care. I grabbed a melting cookie crumb–coated ice pack from my lunch box and pushed it to my temple and eyes, wondering if I'd ever make it back to Prescott's Courthouse Square and stroll under the giant sequoias before I died.

Someone must've called Michelle to inform her of my predicament, but I doubted they were capable, so I called her myself to make sure she was aware of my sudden, mysterious illness. I didn't want to be trapped in this condition in the haunted postal basement, where one guy was spending his lunch hour doing laps inside and outside the building as a workout.

During his routine, the fitness guy realized I was on my back with ice on my face and not delivering mail, taking lunch, or also running in circles around the basement. He stopped and asked, "You OK?"

The sudden attention threw me off. I was a little dizzy from watching the Kentucky Derby training circuit with one aching eye. "Uh, yeah … this heat. And my back. I don't know, maybe I've been taking too much Advil?"

"Huh, yeah, it's hot. That's why I put a soda in the freezer down here," he explained while marching in place before checking his watch and darting to the other room where the fridge was.

I looked at my phone again and called Michelle. "Hey, uh, are you almost done? I'm back at the post office. I'm in the basement, and I have an ice pack."

She answered, obviously driving because the background noise sounded as loud as a rattling coffee can trapped under a car. "I'm almost there. Are you OK? We can leave early."

"Oh, good. Thanks. Motrin or heat—I don't know—got to me. I'll be in the basement with an ice pack."

I suddenly realized that the cookies were still in my lunch box, right next to me, not more than a few minutes after this beneficial information exchange had passed.

"Oh, shit!" My eyes darted around, and I racked my brain to figure out what to do. I quickly opened the lunch box, and the air smelled as strong as a skunk wandering through the azaleas around our house on a dewy summer morning. I slammed the lid shut in a panic. Spotting the nearby trash can, I disposed of the evidence and sprinted back to the couch.

My heart rate began dropping when I overheard the manager approach Michelle as she entered the building upstairs. "There's something wrong with him. He doesn't look very good."

"We're going to leave. I'll take him to urgent care."

She must've been genuinely worried and perplexed, running down the stairs to find me holding an ice pack to my head with one hand and clutching the lunch box in the other, nervously eyeing a talking trash can.

My QUIET, composed, fellow mail-marching life companion and spouse remained calm and focused on our drive to urgent care. I was usually good under pressure, but after spending a dozen years with Michelle, I knew she was exceptionally level-headed in the face of difficult circumstances.

The nurse called my name, so I stood.

"Can she come with me?" I pointed at Michelle, who was wearing an identical uniform.

The nurse nodded, amused and confused. I suspected she wanted to ask me out.

Michelle's presence compelled me to provide clarification. "I should introduce you ..."

I think Michelle interrupted and told the nurse her name, but I'm not sure if anyone figured out we were more than coworkers and that she wasn't some crazy supervisor following me to the doctor to make sure I was too sick to keep working. After all, the post office has a particular reputation.

They positioned the hospital bed against the wall, and the

nurse was short. She reached over and apologized for suffocating me with her generous curves and attached EKG wires all over my body. The nurse asked questions I don't remember because I only recall the stickers feeling sticky and my air supply being briefly cut off, and I was worried that I hadn't brushed my teeth. Embarrassed and trying to suppress a grin, I glanced at Michelle in the chair in the room's corner. She wasn't grinning.

After a few minutes of silence, the doctor entered the room and looked puzzled, probably thinking he was seeing double. *Two* postal employees? I think Michelle explained something about our connection, but I'm not sure. I told the doctor my symptoms, too loopy and distracted to make much sense.

The doctor couldn't find any problems with the EKG or any other administered tests, and he appeared mildly confused. "Did you eat anything unusual? *Drink* anything?"

"Uh, no." I figured it was best to deny everything. The electrolytes-infused beverages given to me by the lovely older lady were reliable and refreshing, but *maybe they got too warm sitting in the mailbox.*

The doctor expressed his cluelessness at my condition, suggesting we agree on a diagnosis relating to some kind of inner-ear anomaly. We all meditated on the possibility for a few seconds, in awkward silence, thanking each other for reasons I don't remember before going our separate ways. I was supposed to follow up with an ear specialist, which I never did, and gladly went home. Eventually, as shrewd as Sherlock, I pieced together the events leading up to that exact moment. After a few days passed, I made these astute observations on one of our evening walks, sharing the truth with my fantastic companion. Eventually, she laughed.

What I learned about the suspicious-cookie day should have prompted me to pursue a more thorough medical review of my condition instead of sobering up with a Sergio Leone movie marathon and a bag of chips. I was told by a few doctors and countless back pain sufferers over two and half years, *back pain is a bitch, and it's usually not that big of a deal, so deal with it.* Even though I figured out after a few hours of sobering up that my spine had not *literally* snapped, I wish I would have figured out what yet another villain may have been making crystal clear. Sometimes, "everyone else" is dead wrong.

HOSPITAL IN BOSTON

THE STRUDEL, THE CAKE, AND THE BRAIN JUICE

JUNE 2021

REGRETTABLY, current events have made it blatantly obvious I was not grasping the true nature of past villains, similar to how doctors do not always comprehend the actual causes of many rare medical conditions. The hospital reprieve provided me with sleepless hours and days to reflect on the past, to "find myself," as someone rich was probably doing at the same time (at some snooty resort) because of pandemic working-from-home burnout. I realized that time abruptly stops when tragedy strikes, and everything that follows is undefined, blurry, or as hazy as a QR code (or when I consume too much hazy UFO ale).

Some Oak Creek on tap sounds perfect right now. I'd happily exchange an IPA for the almond milk, water in a plastic cup, and mediocre fucking coffee that must be the cheap instant stuff resembling dry cat food pebbles.

Call the doctor. Schedule appointments and tests. Consult more doctors. Seek second opinions and pray. Break down and eat all the sugar in the house before making a life-altering decision you hope is right but don't know until after you've made it.

Before I realized it, I was being briefed by an anesthesiologist team while reminiscing about juice in cans and, 24 hours later, subjected to two 100 percent insane hospital roommates. Without knowing how this whirlwind of confusion hit me like a seasonal Phoenix haboob, writing simultaneously distracted *and* organized my reeling mind. I began typing in a draft document in my email on my phone because I couldn't sleep ever since waking up from being knocked out.

TICK. *Tick. Tick.* I watched the clock's hand slowly repeat a perpetual racetrack circuit minute after minute, a subtle reminder that life is short and at any moment my time could be up. Or, if I am a little more fortunate, it will be time for another shot, pill, or spinal fluid evaluation that resembles an urgent racing team working in a pit stop. *This* team, however, wore white coats and probably called for roadside help when they needed a flat tire changed.

Not that I'm complaining.

I couldn't be a doctor if I had to be, even if Michelle's cat depended on it.

The surrounding spectacle was impossible to ignore. The incredulous nature of my unexpected condition remained surreal. Inches away, my pinkish-hued brain fluid floated on a pole in a plastic pouch, measured and recorded hourly. It was as unwelcome a sight as the power steering fluid the Lincoln perpetually drank and pissed out. It also reminded me of something even more nefarious called "cherry juice."

One doctor called it "brain juice," which didn't make me feel more relaxed.

It was very popular with the medical staff, drawing in crowds and demonstrations and reorienting the whole balancing act that the contraption required. The "brain juice contraption" resembled a strange surveyor instrument, complete with a laser level and scale for reference and a few too many valves. Perhaps it better embodied the delicate balance of life and death. Especially if it's beside your bed, and you stare at it for almost an entire week, wishing the view was of blazing maples in autumn from a sad little Ranger or a sexy villainous Lincoln while performing zealous burnouts, with only a few cows and cactus to bear witness.

My focus always returned to the nurse who handed me yet another pill cup, which contained two different varieties of ibuprofen, two doses of narcotics, multiple antibiotics shots, accompanied by a single shot of steroids in my arm. Plus, a muscle-relaxing happy pill that was optional but encouraged with the same indifference as a handful of fortune cookies at any Chinese restaurant. I depleted the cocktail with equal disgust and fascination, mesmerized by my misfortune and the lumbar drain monitored beside my bed.

Is this an acid trip?

I had never consumed acid, but maybe the discount meat thermometer that my skeptical wife had bought a few weeks ago really was crap and the pork was undercooked?

Or is this a twisted Stephen King–X Files–Twilight Zone *trinity nightmare?*

No, that's impossible.

My vision wasn't black-and-white or grainy like a movie shot on old-school nondigital film, and I didn't have trouble hearing dialogue. There was no opening credits magically scrolling in the air across the room, and I didn't hear a narrator, so, no, I couldn't be trapped in a classic horror flick.

There was no Scully around (except for some homeless cat with that name that Michelle was looking to adopt online), so it couldn't have been *The X Files.* Unless the Cigarette Smoking Man in the bed next to me qualified, but that's a stretch and purely coincidental, I think.

Dammit, everything that is happening is as "real" as the "wicked local" dairy and as painful as the 10 minutes after I foolishly consume it.

None of those hollow accusations held any weight, that much was apparent, and as the neurosurgeon stated more than once, I simply succumbed to "bad luck." I'll take that assessment further and say worse luck than when the barista spells your name wrong, the Lincoln's brakes crap out on the highway, or if someone brings gluten-free cookies or beer to a party.

The only cookie I had eaten in recent memory was gifted by a friendly nurse on my birthday, the day after my 10-hour surgery. She also brought me a brownie and a slice of hospital cake since the circumstances were depressing. The surgery took slightly longer than advertised. The extended version, of course, like any good spaghetti Western, international flight, or sleepless night spent staring at hospital ceiling tiles trying to make sense of rock bottom, really fucking bad fucking luck.

JUNE 2010

SOME BIRTHDAYS ARE BETTER than others, but I have a history of absurd and polarizing experiences marking the occasion. The most recent one stole the show for sure, if all previous birthdays were competing and ranked. Spending my birthday in the hospital was not as fun but perhaps as memorable as spending it in Israel 11 years ago, with Michelle and a million street cats. The flight took forever, but the British served plenty of high-altitude tea and coffee, and the destination proved more than worth the inconvenience of jet lag.

The "study abroad" adventure happened during a lull in Middle Eastern conflict, a brief window of opportunity to tour the ancient holy land before ISIS was trending and while Hamas was taking a coffee break. Drinking Turkish coffee in thimbles in Old Jerusalem was satisfying, even though we hadn't seriously picked up the habit yet. I would appreciate that dark, bold, grainy roast more now since I'm not a caffeine poser these days:

I'm an addict or enthusiast (the distinction between the two isn't clear anymore). It was similar to a social smoking gesture, which we also adopted since everyone puffed a pack an hour. We speculated that's how the locals stayed thin and remained calm during times of neighborly geopolitical tension. They were Jewish, so they'd probably live to a hundred without trying anyway. Living every day as if it was their last, the locals we met knew how to live.

Turkish Delight, however, is a misrepresented product and inferior to the coffee. It was as bad as the saltwater taffy they hawked on the Jersey shore boardwalk or the Fruit Roll-Ups we begged for as kids in ShopRite. It differs from Turkish coffee because it can resemble plastic explosives, as the airport security staff reminded me at the Ben Gurion Airport. The security officers were also not delighted to find the Quran I picked up at a bookshop in Jordan and packed next to a tin of extra shekels we couldn't seem to get rid of. That combination probably wasn't kosher.

We cooled off with the piping-hot mislabeled espresso that we eventually replaced with an iced mocha coffee because we were barely adults, taking an intermission from shopping for souvenirs and our joint pedestrian walking tradition. We loved the café's experience and inviting, relaxed atmosphere. This was a desert I could see myself calling home, and now in the hospital, I began to miss it. Sorry, Arizona, I may have to cheat on you if I get the opportunity. The hospitality of everyone we met was as impressive as the sheer number of cats roaming through the Negev. The scenery was of truly biblical proportions, and trading this desert for a remarkably similar Southwest back in the States didn't seem too bad of an idea. Likewise, the produce was as incredible as anything from the Garden State I was used to defending, so you can imagine my disappointment when the DNA test I later took showed zero Jewish heritage.

If there was one lesson I learned during our Israel escapade, it was to live life now, not later. You never know when an Israeli

Defense Forces soldier will accidentally drop a semi-auto clip on your head on the train back from Jerusalem, when your spine will snap, or what the next birthday will bring. Hopefully, the cake marking my 32nd year is as good as the mouthwatering apple strudel they bake in the Old City's Austrian Hospice. Sorry, Boston, your hospital cake scores a zero in my book, but that's not really why I was visiting, so I will let it pass.

VILLAIN NUMBER 8: THE CAT GRAVE

AUGUST 2019

THE MATTRESS DID NOT PERMIT me to sleep past 3 or 4 a.m. anymore. The postal career was taking its expected seasonal toll, and the rally car clutch may have gained a few pounds of resistance. I never became a fitness fanatic or gym rat, but I imagined releasing the clutch was as painful as using a leg press with shinsplints and a snapped tendon. Even though the incredible sports gods play with all kinds of injuries, they have steroids, drugs, and a compensated team of support staff to get them through it and when that strategy doesn't work out, they cheat. Just kidding, they would never do that. My support group was a little more spartan; I only had a perplexed wife and her dying cat.

The glow of the cable TV box cast a variety of shadows on the wavy plaster walls. Sprawled out on the floor, I tried to stretch my overly tight legs and radiating hips. I wondered why the light attached to one wall would turn off and on by itself sometimes. Logical explanations don't go very far in historical residences. All I knew was the house was old enough for a member of the Paul Revere family to have lived there at one point.

Allegedly, anyway. That's if you trust oral historians and family legends hashed out over vodka-spiked punch during a century-old traditional Christmas Eve party.

According to the cane-wielding armchair historians, the room once was "a butchery for pigs," and it used to be painted a brilliant red as if the pigs needed to be memorialized. Now, it was a refreshed, muted green and beige living room slowly transitioning into a cat gymnasium. I don't know what to believe about its dicey past, but I suspect that a ghost pig is heavier underfoot than a cat, which might explain why it sounded like something was always walking around in the kitchen around the corner. I hoped all the ghosts knew I was only a mailman, not a butcher. Hence the typical fear-induced midnight prayer session: *"Please don't get revenge on the guy delivering the bills. I swear I don't eat bacon at Sunday breakfast—I give mine to the fat cat. He's in the cellar right now. Go haunt him."*

The floors easily creaked, and the three cats could effortlessly disturb the old planks, except two of them were always sleeping in the cellar early in the morning. So it couldn't have been them. They were probably chasing mice in their dreams; they were so well fed that I don't think they put much effort into curtailing the rodent population. Regardless of these distractions, I remained frustrated that the incorrect lifting, repetition, lack of conditioning, stress, or whatever the hell I was doing wrong was affecting my life so profoundly. My back would flare up to the point where I was talking to a cat at 4 a.m., or praying on the floor that the "demon pigs" would lose to a battle with "Fat Silver" downstairs, hoping Paul Revere's ancestors were friendly to people from New Jersey who were of German heritage but not Hessian, I think.

Living in a CONEX box in St. Johns, Arizona sounded appealing, but there is very little to no coffee scene.

The cat I called Juniper wasn't a cellar dweller because she didn't get along with the other cats. Her proper Christian name was something I honestly forgot. She reminded me of the Alligator juniper out west that lived for a few hundred years and had a distinct rugged appearance. I bet the other two cats didn't want to be around her because she was as temperamental as Jezebel in pursuit of the prophet Elijah. If she was a dog, I'd call her a bitch, but since she's a cat, I guess she's a queen. The other two tomcats were weary suffering under her reign, with not so much as a cat tree to take shelter. Her vehement hissing and howling matched the ferociousness of a lynx.

JUNIPER'S DEMONS were many and unforgiving, especially at night. It seemed we were both plagued by the same affliction. Whenever I was pacing around, stretching, or grabbing another ice pack, she would show up out of nowhere and incessantly howl. I had enough problems to deal with, but she must've thought the same about her situation because she liked to relay her issues by yodeling. Perhaps, though, she just wanted attention; I swear I don't know that much about cats.

The vocal-prone feline would alternate between making two sounds: a shrill purr with a rolled "r" and an abrupt nasal cough, to solicit attention more than to clear the throat. Maybe it annoyed her that I was making too much noise. I don't know what she was thinking, but eventually her thin toothpick frame would wander over to me, and the coughing and howling would cease if I patted her fragile-looking head. I guess some company is better than none sometimes. We would observe the supernatural phenomenon together, only at that place and red-eye time because we were suffering, even though we both didn't know from what.

"What's wrong, Juniper? You look great."

"Praroop!"

"Are you hungry?"

"Praroop!"

"Are you sick?"

"Ah-guh!"

"I don't know why this hurts again. I thought I was lifting correctly. Must be the mail or that mattress."

"Praroop!"

"Fucking rally cars."

"Ah-guh!"

"Maybe you need more food or something. I bet the other cats are stealing."

The "house" would usually interrupt these exchanges. The walls would make noise, the floors would resume their creaks, and the chairs at the kitchen table would sound like someone was trying to find the best one even though they all sucked. *Should we have added cushions?*

It was amid a bout of musical chairs or industrious mouse carpentry that I'd try to fall asleep on the couch with an ice pack and pain pill bottle. *The Twilight Zone* was creeping me out, Ken Burns was narrating something for five hours straight, or an infomercial was solving vitamin deficiencies. Sometimes I would fall back asleep, and when I did, the attention-hogging cat would cough and march away in a huff. Usually, that's when the milk delivery person would arrive, rattling glass bottles outside, or when the doughnut shop's dumpster across the street was being emptied. My father-in-law would show up with a strict weather-dependent deadline and crank up the news at maximum volume to hear the forecast because of a distrust of cellphone apps. I would soon be awake again, running on fumes, fumbling with pour-over coffee cone filters that looked like upside-down pyramids, trying to get amped for yet another round of the devil's march. But first, I'd check some stocks because delusional day-trade scheming dulls the sting of reality. This routine would occur more often and with little warning, because sometimes I would feel as high as the Nasdaq.

It must be the weather, the heavy clutch, the mail volume, the coffee roll I shouldn't have eaten, or maybe the tide, I would speculate while observing the phases of the moon, listening to the sound-track of a paranormal opera performing an encore.

One thing, though, *was* for sure. I was never getting much sleep, probably sounding like an unintelligible hyperthyroid cat with a personality disorder and throat tick.

MICHELLE TOLD me she thought I was unique when she first met me. Not rare or "wicked smart," just different from the typical Boston sports addict chugging energy drinks and specialty coffee, constantly waving tickets for a game.

"Was he quietly intelligent beyond his years? Mysterious like Fox Mulder? Or was this blind, true love?"

Michelle asked these questions early in our relationship, convinced the answer was yes, all the above. She thought I had the capacity for growth, though, but I only recall being preoccupied with sweet-sounding exhaust systems and figuring out how dark I could get away with tinting the windows. She recognized the long-term potential, once sharing that she valued my ability to learn from mistakes, a rare attribute.

However, one conversation nearly changed her admirable view of me. It was, of course, about cats. Michelle was a lifelong animal lover and feline enthusiast. I call her the "mother of cats," even though she prefers "protector of the kittie babies." Convinced that God had predestined her to help them all live out their nine lives to their absolute fullest potential, she was a big fan of the devious rodent-loving animals, despite my apprehension. After exhaustively narrating the backgrounds of the three cats she left back home in Massachusetts, she asked me one question I forgot but instantly knew I had answered incorrectly.

"Yeah, but you know they don't have souls, right?" The words escaped my mouth, and I regretted not biting my tongue.

She was floored. Shocked. Angry. Hurt.

I was almost single again, and annoyed that I had pointed out such a stupid, insensitive fact. The innocent Boston girl had told me about one of the most important aspects of her life, and I had brushed it off with the arrogance of an 18-year-old. I had no experience with cats or any real pets, and in my defense, the only dogs I remember were on TV. Growing up, we had a bird who died trying to lay an egg and a goldfish that displayed suicidal tendencies, yet somehow lived forever. The fish's name was Goldie because its appearance and our snack of choice inspired my sister. Goldie threw rocks at the glass tank all night because it did not appreciate captivity, or maybe its adopted name. I fed it more than a Nano Pet, so I don't think I was to blame for its aggressive behavior. Luckily, Michelle was not aggressive toward me after hearing the ill-timed theory about cat souls, and in some ways, I've since become reformed.

I FIRST MET the now-deceased cat during a period in its Methuselah-challenging, world-record-contending life that could be labeled as "post-prime." I won't sugarcoat my initial uneducated view of cats. It was one of avoidance and slight disgust. When digging a cat's grave, it is critical to remember to disguise emotional detachment, with the reverie that genuine admirers expect and display during such a solemn ceremony. I tried to respect the event, but the weather was humid, and the parched mosquitoes were savage. The job was as exhausting as dirty.

The night was muggy, and I remember the moon glaring down on us, hinting that New England's macabre lure was verifiable and if I buried the animal incorrectly or with the wrong attitude, a curse would be placed on my soul. Organic bug spray was defective against the gnat vampires, and my half-naked legs were fair game. Decked out in our unchanged ink-stained postal uniforms, supplied with flashlights and shovels, I, my wife, and her mom committed to laying the noble animal to rest as best we could in the dark while being eaten alive.

After scouting out a few potential locations, I picked a spot to dig the pit, realizing that all the yard was as rocky as the Granite

Dells I missed exploring, not fertilized, loamy topsoil. The shovel's metallic ring at every stab at the earth turned the task bleak, and I announced to the two participants in mourning that this venture would require substantially laborious shoveling. My patience was running out quicker than my energy, and I could have waited for my brother-in-law to fire up the tractor with the correct attachment for digging, but that plan seemed like overkill. Besides, I was a "real man" who could dig a hole since I had worked on a farm after graduating from excavating sandcastle moats during my formative years. I was more than physically capable, even blowing off the chiropractor since the beginning of the summer. My back was improving due to all the walking, hamstring stretching, ice, heat, positive thinking, and occasional ibuprofen popping when it sporadically flared up.

In all sincerity, I was despondent for the dying cat while she waited in line to enter the pearly gates. It seemed like a slow, painful, protracted existence the veterinary experts had attempted to delay with advanced medications and lifestyle modifications. The shots didn't seem to provide much relief. The liquid syringes barely contacted her angry pursed lips, and the prescription-style food looked as appealing as a plant-based burger. I swear she despised my presence despite offering her wild captain-cut salmon. The bribes didn't work. After all, *I* was the intruder, the newcomer. Juniper had lived in that house longer than Michelle and I had been acquainted.

There were some evenings when poor old Juniper would pace up and down the creaky stairs, providing a ghostly presence to the already haunted historical house. At least my wife and I evaded being banished to the cellar or attic, where I'm sure paranormal episodes occurred as frequently as sitcom reruns on the antenna channels. I have my in-laws to thank for that. *At least they had not suggested a more hazardous location than our cramped, single-windowed cat-box-sized room.*

· · ·

THE SHOVEL WAS A TYPICAL ONE, stout, wooden, old, and stored in the cellar for most of the year until it was time to attempt tomato growing or bury something that had unexpectedly expired. I couldn't help but hit every buried rock, eventually working hard enough to provide an ample-sized hole fitting for a majestic feline that graced her family for nearly two decades. Until that moment, I thought cats lived for around five years (about the age of our stack of dead laptops) before being run over or abandoned. If age wasn't a factor, maybe disillusioned owners returned them to shelters, or they ran away to live in dumpsters. Her existence and ultimate demise proved educational, but I became convinced her gray-white skittish and dementia-plagued apparition also haunted me soon after digging the burial hole.

Just a few days after her passing, the pain in my back had magically returned, howling with a vengeance.

HOSPITAL IN BOSTON
THE PHOENIX LIGHTS

JUNE 2021

THE NURSE MAY HAVE HELD my hand or arm or both to be nice when another woman whose credentials I forgot pulled the drain out of my back, but I'm not sure my memory was accurate. Something burned, and I was busy grinding my teeth. It's a good thing there wasn't anything reflective on the walls or Michelle was around. Now I know why there are never-ending shower curtains surrounding the beds in hospital rooms, but my eyes were half-closed, anyway. We talked about pizza shops because she was going to Phoenix for a vacation, and although the conversational distraction was helpful, it didn't put me at ease. Though, the drugs were mellowing my imagination, because if my senses were as sharp as the staple the "other woman" was trying to insert, I may have passed out during the procedure.

2009

I ONCE COPILOTED a Cessna 172 into Sky Harbor Airport, in Phoenix, *at night*, not to have a pizza but because my airsick flight instructor suffered from boredom and was a little crazy. I may as well have been blindfolded, with very few hours logged. We were in a holding pattern between 737s and other large aircraft waiting to get clearance to land. There was no clear or satisfactory reason for doing this other than bragging rights, and they weren't for me. *I just wanted the license.*

I was in this predicament because, as a freshman in college, I was overly ambitious and ready to take risks, traits I attribute to my firstborn status. Considering I had little experience, I was good at piloting a single-engine aircraft on short notice once arriving at the flight school in Arizona. Undeniably a kid, at 18, I only had minimal experience driving a car and a farm truck. All things considered, I was doing reasonably well balancing aviation, academics, fast food, a hot girlfriend, and living away from home. It was challenging but satisfying to learn a new skill that required precision. The best part of the adventure was that I would become a licensed pilot after completing the program, which is not something everyone can claim. Some licensed drivers can barely navigate four wheels on asphalt without losing the privilege or control while taking a stoned selfie.

Besides the absurd night flight, my first solo cross-country trip was the most life-threatening experience I can remember. My destination was Flagstaff, a small high-altitude airport on a mountain, where the weather was precarious and notably windy. I should have abandoned the landing altogether, but I was inexperienced, so I committed to the "touch and go" for no reason other than wanting to get it over with. The air traffic controller must've developed immediate ulcers at my decision, as the plane rocked back and forth, worried the Cessna's approach was coming in too fast and too high.

"Easy, *easy*," he announced into my headset.

I realized the wind was too many knots for my level of expertise, and it didn't matter if I had nailed the landing before because the airplane bounced onto the runway momentarily instead of permanently. Briefly airborne again, I floated over the pavement for what seemed like an eternity before somehow leveling out. The plane shuddered, the tires kissed the airstrip with a jolt, and I think the traffic control voice in my ear said something congratulatory. The celebration was quickly over, and I throttled the lucky Cessna down the tarmac, ready to fly to the next airport for another touch and go before returning to my flight school to complete the mission.

I pulled off the incredible stunt and finished the program by the end of my college freshman year, receiving an FAA-issued license in the mail shortly after arriving in New Jersey. Our mailman liked to throw our mail into the box; rumor was they enrolled him in an anger management course. *I now understand why.* But that one foreboding landing was the closest call and the most terrified I had ever been since experiencing the boardwalk clowns and, more recently, after reading radiology reports.

THE HOSPITAL WAS a constant reminder of close calls and dysphoria. My second roommate was in awful shape, sounded as loud as a clown, but was not funny or entertaining to listen to. His phone calls to distant family members who preferred virtual visits were depressing. They reminded me of flying through the desert with aviator sunglasses and a leather jacket. The better times when I was carefree yet scared of failing grades, an unfinished pilot's license, and that all future cars would be electric and ruin an enthusiast's dream of rowing through a sweet five-speed transmission.

The roommate's aches, pains, and nicotine-withdrawal fits always ruined my recollections. The horrifying thing is, this guy's bleak existence was one case out of millions, held together by fewer threads than the sutures sewed into my back. From what I could gather, the diagnosis was grim: a fractured hip, broken leg, cancer fucking everywhere, and COPD. Such a fate wouldn't have me checking in for surgery, upset that the rehab clinic didn't have a bed for me. I think I'd call a cab, head to the border wall with a MAGA hat, and cocaine brick, make a scene, and pray I would get caught in the crossfire of some epic cartel versus border patrol standoff.

Fuck oxygen machines bitching all night, urinals, bedsores, cancer, miserable hospital food. I'd prefer to go out with some dignity and excitement. It sounded more appealing than a perpetual hospital existence. Why look forward to a mushy meal delivered on a rolling cart instead of a nice steak and a bottle of wine? Or even a "double-double animal style" burger with fries and a shake, lactose villains be as damned as all the other unjust consorts. *God, I miss those.* However, anything is probably better than the hospital fare; they run out of dinner rolls and routinely forget the pudding spoon.

VILLAIN NUMBER 9: THE DEVIL'S MARCH

2015-2021

MY BIASED WIFE assures me black cats are "good luck," especially if you live in Massachusetts, where most luck has been captured and chained to someone's trust fund, probably dating back to a Mayflower relative. I'm sure this belief has nothing to do with Michelle growing up with a black cat, and glued to *Sabrina the Teenage Witch*, now wishing our lives were narrated by a witty cat providing some '90s-themed levity to the current stalemate. Those are the innocent, harmless white lies I'd wager *won't* kill me. However, walking a beat for several miles five or six days a week for a few decades can't be good for your health.

There's no variety.

I've been told otherwise by delusional proponents of unbalanced power walking over the past few years, but those theories sound as palatable as propaganda from Y2K. Yeah, sure, grappling a few pounds of sooty paper-cut-prone correspondence with an ink-stained left arm is good for the joints. I beg to differ, and I'm calling the blatant lie out. It's a scam. Repetition *must* take its toll in all of its unhealthy forms, just as sitting replaced smoking and vaping replaced glue or hairspray or whatever people in the '80s did, which replaced cocaine the D.A.R.E. officer informed us his "friends" considered remarkable in the '70s.

You know the hokey jingle people like to recite when they see a letter carrier fumbling through the route on a shitty day (rain, shine, blah blah). The mail must go through! Why? I don't know. It's mostly discarded solicitations, I think. Despite a growing list of reservations, I found creative ways to overcome the ridiculous obstacles, probably because of my work ethic, a fear of getting in trouble for skipping deliveries, and my still very unsenior seniority.

AFTER WITNESSING three black cats on my route in a single day I panic dialed my wife, and I swear I wasn't smoking any hash. The omen was as welcome as the typical desperate and broke drug addict asking me if I had their "check" yet. Nonetheless, that kind of repetition didn't seem coincidental. Perhaps the cat sighting was foreshadowing a career spent lugging heavy flyers on top of my left arm while juggling magazines and a dozen maraca-sounding medications in my satchel.

Michelle assured me I was probably just paranoid.

Regardless, I felt like a government sponsored drug dealer weighed down by fat coupon books and past-due electric bills. I'm not surprised that postal employees used to chain-smoke in the office in the morning before they started their routes or "coke it up" in Florida when they retired. The job will wear you out quicker than shoe soles that disintegrate within three months of consecutive mail marching. I should've guessed without the internet sages that the trio of cats was warning me that the villains were catching up to me again. *I probably should've known, but I honestly don't know that much about cats.*

I would usually consider Michelle a person of reputable judgment and a good influence in my life. The *only* influencer I subscribe to, really. She is as honest as Abe Lincoln, but I'm probably biased since she's my wife and I used to drive a Lincoln. However, she also introduced me to the postal system— a strange, outdated, debt ridden enterprise brimming with toxicity and not a cent of common sense.

Before joining the ranks, the only time I had entered a post office as an adult was to get my passport to "study abroad" with my future spouse. However, after about four years of pounding the pavement, the significant wear and tear seemed to cause cumulative and permanent damage to my body. The career choice may have been as unwise as a bottle of absinthe and was definitely nowhere near as much fun as getting my passport stamped one particularly drunk summer.

They called us "letter *carriers*," but "letter-delivering *characters*" is a more appropriate designation. At first, I enjoyed the outside job, its related challenges, and time constraints that quickly made the day go by, but what else could I do? Besides, if you had the right frame of mind and sufficient energy, and ran through the routes, the adrenaline rush hinted you were taking part in a marathon like an athlete. Sometimes you thought you were in the Olympics. People would hand you frozen water bottles in the summer when commenting on the ridiculous uniform shorts, and homemade cookies or a Fireball nip in the winter, cheering you on.

———

THEY DID NOT ASSIGN us any hazard pay, but they should have.

The sleepy, overcast afternoon was misty and typically monotonous. I was thinking of a coffee nap when a grayish silhouette darted across the road as I turned a corner, and I instinctively halted. *Was that a dog? No, it was too big and quick. Besides, this was a trailer park, and there were breed limitations and weight rules. Coyote? No, it was too gray. Turkey? No, he must be dead by now. I hadn't seen him for a few weeks, and the stringy bird wasn't quick or gray. Huh, how odd.*

After a slight hesitation and rescheduled coffee break, I continued the route, remaining more alert for the rest of the day, worried a skin-walker was roaming the grounds and my family's unproven whispers of distant Seneca ancestry were accurate. If a stray dog was loose and rabid, I was afraid my fate would be as gruesome as the horror stories of dog bite injuries or fatalities that made headlines every year. Luckily, all the pet dogs on my route were small, harmless, and friendly.

The turkey, however, was no one's pet, friend, or companion. It was as huggable as a teddy bear cholla, as confident as a cactus wren, and as hotheaded as all of my uncles. The wiry, sad son of a bitch lived another day to be a pestering asshole, probably suffering from some kind of mental condition or loneliness. The animal control officers even wanted nothing to do with it, although I protested for months about how it would chase me and harass everything in its path. It would perch on a porch or on top of a mailbox with the confidence of a tiger, shrieking its "gobble" yodel with the vigor of something possessed. Every chance it spotted me with one of its cocked bouncing eyes, it would direct a barrage of noise and attitude at me, and about half the time, puff up his feathers and chase me down the street.

At least I had a high-quality satchel and was wearing the correct shoes, bizarre postal uniform double standards being as convoluted as the inaccurate sizing charts and uncomfortable footwear.

I became accustomed to this ordeal, adapting my route based on the location of the lonely bird. This strategy was inconvenient but my only option. On days when the disturbed foul would camp out under a bird feeder or a porch, I would skip ahead to the next street and hope he had moved by the time I circled back, or at least wouldn't be there the following day. Sometimes, the bird would muster enough strength to defy gravity and land on someone's mobile home roof because it was probably sick of being yelled at by angry senior citizens trying to access their magazines or coupon flyers. One day, though, the bird disappeared. In retrospect, *maybe it was eaten.*

I REMEMBER COMMUTING one particular day with Michelle, because we worked at the same post office (somehow, that's the only post office that would hire us). The radio interrupted my musings about paper cuts and heavy mail, and a familiar voice sounded over the crackling speakers. It was hard to hear over the bassy rally car exhaust and accompanying turbo whistle.

"Hey, turn that up."

Michelle cranked up the volume knob, and I tried not to step on the gas.

The reporter was interviewing a person who was assaulted by a rabid coywolf. I was shocked. I swore I had seen the animal they described a few days before, and the sudden unexplainable absence of the turkey somehow seemed explainable.

"Wow, it could have attacked me. I guess I don't look as appetizing as a turkey."

Michelle may have agreed but I couldn't hear her response, since the addictive turbo kicked back in, and I made some excellent time.

Over the next couple weeks, I remained extra cautious delivering near any wooded areas of my route, convinced some hybrid dog beast lurked in the brush waiting to pounce. I assumed it was probably thinking of getting revenge on the humans responsible for killing its rabid family patriarch. I also considered how delivering mail in a *Jumanji* universe was perhaps not worth the risks. Especially if my back continued to act up, which meant I wouldn't be able to run away from an attacking werewolf. Contemplating playing the lottery one day, I also wondered how effective a standard issue can of dog spray would be if my life depended on it.

Michelle entertained that question, too, so she tested a can of the stuff out in the driveway on our return home one evening.

Somehow, it caught my eye because liquid mace can be carried downwind. Although the chemical burned profusely, and I ran in circles cursing for a few minutes, I couldn't see how it would save my ass from what the police taser couldn't. Maybe I needed a German Shepherd to help me deliver my route because I kept rolling a five or an eight in this stupid strategy game.

THE CORPORATE MESSAGES sent to the scanner were supposedly written by real people. It was frustrating and unclear if they ever delivered the mail, knew much about the business, or were just aspiring sketch writers hoping to land a gig on a late-night show.

"Drink plenty of fluids."

"Stay out of the sun."

"Take plenty of breaks."

"Consume enough calories."

"Hold the handrail when walking up the stairs."

"Prevent rollaways and runaways. Park your truck with the hand brake set and curb the wheels and shut the vehicle off when you exit it."

"Don't let a dog bite you. Use your satchel as a shield."

"Don't stay in one position too long."

"Pretend you're a robot and save us from bankruptcy."

The last one-liner wisdom nugget is not verbatim, but who would know? The pathetic messages would be mildly funny if they didn't conflict with the "safety talks" that wasted time and stirred up debate every morning. The script was as painful as third bundles, as predictable and cheap as a third-class flyer.

"STATIONARY EVENTS are when your breaks are too long, and they make us look bad; travel time doesn't count toward your breaks. Go faster because our office times are as bad as our street times, but don't go fast if the sidewalk has wet leaves or ice because that's not safe and terrible for our workers' comp office. You should be out delivering already, but none of the mail and parcels are ready for you guys yet because the clerks are under-staffed, have a better union, or are taking lunch at 9 a.m. Or the plant is holding up the truck because their priority is to take lunch. Stop tripping and slipping and falling because route hazards are avoidable somehow, and don't get dehydrated because that's what your breaks are for. We are probably short on vehicles because they are older than the internet and always breaking or catching on fire or rolling away. Just make sure you scan everything because the competition might take all our busi-ness away if we keep missing scans. Don't worry; politicians are not trying to get rid of us, we think. But we will have to merge routes eventually because of all the bad times, and by the way, the algorithm predicts everyone has downtime. Have a safe day."

IF THERE IS one word that sends a postal employee into a rage, it is *downtime*—the singular word selected by managers (or the omniscient algorithm running the place) to describe the "extra time" they predict a route to have. However, it conveniently doesn't mention when it shows you are going *over* eight hours, which is every day from Black Friday to New Year's Eve. So, yeah, convoluted postal math is as rigged as a casino or a lottery, and I guess it makes sense that's the place I ended up working for—it was fate. And that is why everyone is so outraged during "safety talks" that usually end with "and we are going to give everyone a piece of another route because, you know, the "matrix" algorithm predicts everyone has a downtime."

The fucking "matrix" is running the post office, and I'm not surprised. That might be why it doesn't work very well anymore —it's from the 90's. *Maybe it needs a reboot?*

Commence the employee rebellion. Everyone complains about something relevant to the talk, their lack of downtime, or what they were planning to have for lunch if they have enough time to eat it. I was only thinking about how my back would feel if I wasn't delivering such a heavy bundle of mail, and if popping ibuprofen was technically a break, downtime, or a metaphorical blue or red pill.

———

MANAGEMENT LOVES A "RUNNER," as the union officials often scold, which is one of those younger, newer kids who "probably skip breaks or lunches," running mail around town faster than they should. They often warned us about those type of short-lived employees because they are the ones prone to injury and dog bites. Those kind of carriers never lasted long. Somebody probably fired them before making "regular" status due to safety violations.

Like most new, delusional recruits, I started out too ambitious and quick. It didn't take long to realize that game plan led to fatigue and being overburdened with not just your route's mail but someone else's too. That someone else was a veteran carrier who was more tired than you, had health issues, was a union official, or who had too much vacation time carried over from the previous year. Maybe they'd be healthier if they went home early to play golf, or were stricken by a sudden allergic reaction to the rain. Although I may seriously need to enroll in the witness protection program for writing these observations, when your life is upheaved by a rare disease, some things don't seem important anymore, like downtime, the shifty matrix, or, wait for it, *junk mail.*

There, I said it. Heretic, I know!

Ineffectively run bureaucratic organizations staffed by select coworkers who take advantage of union contract fine print deserve a few insults. *Now the union is indeed sending an assassin out to get me, but hopefully, they use snail mail. I've probably got a week's head start on them. I'll be in Arizona sipping something cool and robust, maybe hiding from the postal villains at a wellness retreat, staring at natural mountains and birds that are much nicer than mountains of parcels and bitchy GPS enabled scanners.*

Coffee breaks are a regular part of my life, and I need lunch after walking 10 miles a day, so I can positively say I followed most of the rules and did the job the best I could. Most postal employees probably do, but there's always going to be a few rotten apples, as the saying goes, who sit at a bar in their uniform all day, as the profession is portrayed on TV. Most people running, slowly shuffling, or driving the mail and parcels around were hardworking Americans hoping to do better than their relatives who lived in basements. I just wanted to be outside, getting some exercise and fresh air, attempting to pay off student loans and save for an actual house instead of a tiny free bedroom in a haunted home overrun by immortal cats.

The job seemed to wear me down right when I bought the rally car.

Coincidence? Or were the villains collaborating, forming some kind of evil alliance?

I couldn't understand *why* because I took all the siestas the union bitched about, wasn't running around anymore, and drank all the water I was encouraged to thanks to the morning "safety" meetings. Michelle and I even sometimes splurged, taking a few days off to visit the Granite State or Maine to relax. The rugged vacations and frigid air didn't seem to help, though, and with my escalating pain I was convinced I would never make it to retirement and Florida's Nalcrest community.

The repetition became unbearable. Walk another "loop," pop another pain pill, drink another coffee, or eat a coffee roll to distract myself from a monotonous reality. I felt trapped in one of those unending vortex slinky-shaped spirals I used to draw with a number two pencil in the corner of a book when trying to stay awake in middle school since the official outcome of winning paper football was a demerit. However, the only result of delivering the route seemed like pain. The 10-mile-a-day mail drudgery became my villain as I trudged through the snow, ice, hurricanes, and dark with a headlamp and a limp, "walking off" the pain so that I could continue the brutal devil's march.

Maybe I wasn't consuming enough protein, water, or perhaps *too much* coffee? Did I need a more leisurely route, or an entirely different job because I was somehow very weak? The questions filled my head until I publicly acknowledged the off-and-on chronic pain in my back and leg I had been experiencing for two years. Even the most selfish coworkers and oblivious managers became concerned. This encouraged everyone to share their "war stories" of slipped disks, herniated spines, broken hips and legs, carpal tunnel syndrome, arthritis, pinched nerves, sciatica, alcoholism, PTSD, and mental breakdowns. The place was as dismal as Shutter Island or a clinic for people with physical disabilities who kept working through everything, so I shrugged off the pain, ingested more pills, or called out sick.

Everyone in the profession had some kind of ailment, so maybe I was actually exaggerating or as delicate as a desert brittlebush. Perhaps I was getting older or slowly walking too fast. The real reason didn't surface until much later, but even when the pain would subside after a weekend, vacation, or sick day, it predictably returned when I returned to my route. Maybe this devil's march was my real villain, as it is for many of its victims who put up with hauling around catalogs, newspapers, and cat litter ordered online by socially anxious basement gamers day after day after day after day over their entire repetitious careers.

DELIVER the mail in temperatures under 32 degrees and try not to curse the weather or the profession. The snow was piling on the windshield, and it froze the stiff wiper blades to the glass. The conditions were perilous, and the little "iron duke" engine was having difficulty starting when it was this cold.

I was unsurprised.

The aging appliance on wheels was carbureted since the fleet of mail trucks was older than me. I guess you could register it as an antique if you were stupid enough to buy one at a government auction, but be warned, they have a tendency to combust spontaneously. Given their undesirable driving characteristics, I don't think you'll see one at a collector car auction in the future; you might as well burn your extra cash to keep warm or visit Scottsdale and blow it all at the adult clubs lining the way to a Barrett-Jackson auction. It would be foolish to waste even a dollar on a long-life vehicle (LLV) with basically no heat.

Some manufacturers and business fleets adequately equipped vehicles for driving through winter storms, but the LLV was good only at getting stuck or nearly getting me killed. Swinging the ice scraper across the glass, I circled the truck to clear as much snow as possible before jumping back inside and slamming the sliding door shut. Settling into the seat, I threw the gloves onto the dash and held my hands up to the two air vents that were barely blasting warm air. Everything was painted white outside, as the blowing snow accumulated faster than the weather alerts on my phone, which I suddenly realized was missing. I checked my pocket, the tray of mail, the floor, the scanner holder–turned–cupholder, and the mail satchel. Panic set in as I stared out at the blizzard, wondering if I had dropped it on my last attempt to deliver frozen mail.

Without the phone, I was potentially stranded. What if I need to call for help? The truck might not start or decide to go up in flames. Sometimes the seat belt would trap you and need to be cut. The scanner would die because batteries don't last in the cold. Or what if a dog launched an attack? I doubt any animal would venture out in whiteout conditions, but the threat of porch pirates was genuine, and I suspected aliens abducted the pack of coywolves that probably ate the turkey. The threats were endless, and without a phone, it would be as analog as the '90s again, except I was too young to know how to survive as an adult back then because I was only a kid. I guess you'd have to memorize phone numbers or cart around a phone book, but good luck finding a pay phone; Amazon parcel lockers replaced them at our local convenience store. Very helpful.

I don't know what was worse: driving the LLV through a snowstorm or the Ranger in any kind of weather. At least in the Ranger, we drove somewhere worth going. We'd often dedicate Sunday sabbaticals to relaxing because studying, road-tripping, and worrying about future careers throughout the week can be incredibly tiring. Michelle and I would pick up a good half dozen since calories were still disposable and head up to a park that was empty early on the weekend, before the families and their minivans would roll in and unpack fur-babies or children. While the sun was rising we would eat breakfast Bavarian-style, watching the irradiated butte and contrasting towering conifers that evoked our origins back in the Northeast. I won't lie, we missed the tall woods which are commonplace in Jersey or Massachusetts; the grass always seems greener on the other side of the hill. Sometimes, though, the greener side is as fake as the turf at a football game and as comforting as delivering mail in a rattle-can death trap with rust holes in the floor, but where else are the doughnut crumbs supposed to go? You keep the mail clean if you're a real professional.

ALTHOUGH HINDSIGHT CAN DISTORT, I'd bet a book of stamps that staring at a butte eating a doughnut is nicer than watching a catalog I dropped get swept across the street of a trailer park during a New England blizzard. *Maybe the grass isn't greener back in Arizona, as my unreliable mind's eye wants to portray it?* No, to be honest, analogies are probably subconscious attempts to justify what we already know. Nothing more than patinas—thinly veiled, convenient excuses for remorsefulness. If the grass really *was* greener marching through postal hell, I wouldn't have tripped on ice, landed on my tailbone a dozen times, or have been borderline frostbitten, wishing I hadn't lost my phone because I distinctly remember being pissed I couldn't check the weather forecast in a much more agreeable Tempe.

Fuck the grass anyway. I'm allergic. A stone-covered sandbox lined with rocks, wiry gravel ghosts, and riddled with lizards to laugh at must be at least 50 degrees better. I know because I experienced it once, back before the initial Lincoln's curse started my vicious spiral to the crabgrass tundra hell where I was drowning in endless trays of junk mail and trudging through mindless, wearisome loops.

HOSPITAL IN BOSTON

LEAKS ARE BAD

JUNE 2021

SLEEPING on my burning back in an elevated hospital bed, with the music from my headphones resonating in my ears, I was relieved to drift away into a world that didn't exist. My wearied brain was overloaded and my body fatigued, victims of sleep deprivation and major surgery. Eventually, an overwhelmed system automatically shifts into a critical mode when it reaches its limit. The relaxing pills, "sleeping playlists," and counting of villain-sheeps were not doing the trick, and something in my head suddenly announced, "checking out."

I wasn't just deprived of sleep over the past few years. Despite uncertain careers, the one goal Michelle and I sought to accomplish since graduating from microwave dinners and Cornish game hens cooked in toaster ovens was self-sufficiency, *together*. It's funny how sometimes you have to claw uphill to get what you want, realizing when you go there, the road ends, and from that vantage point and perspective, the prize has moved to where you began.

Yeah, if we had dropped out of school and stayed in cactus land where it was affordable, less humid, and allergy-free, our lives would be so much better. I should've bought noise-canceling headphones to tune out the world. My life would be drastically altered. There would be no student loans, ridiculous mortgages, insane cost-of-living expenses, and maybe one snow shovel instead of an arsenal.

We were responsible in our younger days—*too responsible.* Michelle and I were also too impressionable by the previous generation's perspective, convinced diplomas were worth any cost and dropping out of school was for quitters. Now I know that what works for some people doesn't work for everyone, and my only regret is not doing what I knew was best for myself instead of listening to what others thought was best for me. The cruel reality of an unpredictable future littered with countless roadblocks can force some people to give up, give in, or take endless detours for the rest of their lives.

Maybe it took us years to make any progress, and perhaps it might all vanish because of spinal-bound shape-shifter villains, but at least I knew one thing I wanted—to be with Michelle.

Many people never know what they want or pursue meaningless things such as staged houses or popularity, until they have that "wake-up call," when they suddenly realize what's important and what's actually stupid. I can't say I'm one of those people. Usually, I know what is essential and sarcastically call out what I believe isn't, and that's probably why I'm not the most popular guy in the room or why my best friend is also my wife.

Our life plan was vague and simple, more relaxed than calculating or superficial. We didn't go out of the way to ruin anyone else's lives, dropping the clutch in front of someone's manicured lawn or asking for a bailout like all the reckless financial institutions that tanked the year we began college. I don't recall crying, accepting charity, or behaving as selfishly as a particular Southwest state that we witnessed *repaving* perfectly smooth roads in the post–Great Recession bailout bonanza era. We were too nice and impressionable. It seemed like after endless roadblocks and nonsensical repaving detours, when we finally overcame the struggle to reach the top of the hill, I was stabbed in the back by an invisible asshole who just wanted a good laugh.

––––––––––

My EYES OPENED, and I saw the white-coat neurology team surrounding me, and they were not laughing. Someone tapped my arm, attempting a late-night "wake-up call." The team paused their open discussion about possible "leaks" when they knew I was awake.

"How are you feeling?" one of them asked.

The question forced me to squint, eyes heavy, at the cast of assembled doctors.

"Fine, I guess."

Until I just woke up and realized something might be awry. Now I'm as petrified as those glassy amber-colored rocks littered around eastern Arizona.

"We just wanted to make sure you are OK. The nurse called us about the drain possibly leaking."

They began discussing an MRI or CT scan, and I couldn't do anything except lie there praying nothing was catastrophically wrong. Hopefully, I wouldn't wind up as dead as poor ole Juniper.

Figures. I finally fall asleep, and everything goes to shit.

The team left with the same urgency as when they had arrived, discussing their unclear plan of action, reassuring me they were working on figuring out what to do. Somehow, the room was quiet again. Perhaps the roommate was content dreaming about going out for a smoke, and somehow I was drowsy enough to fall back asleep. I didn't wake up again until the following day, informed that everything was probably fine. I'd have to stay in the hospital longer so that they could monitor things, specifically that my spinal fluid wasn't leaking out of my back. Because, as they reminded me, that would be bad.

VILLAIN NUMBER 10: THE RELAXING RENOVATION

AUGUST 2021

"Where do I put all these dead, bloated rats?"

MICHELLE ASKED THE HYPOTHETICAL QUESTION, and I stared out the window, speechless. The grass was green, the tomato garden was bursting thanks to a stormy summer, and the ancient pear tree in the middle of the yard was loaded with juicy ripe fruit. The pears littered the ground, the crows liked to knock them down, even though I had already filled a reused drywall bucket with chewed-up remnants and disposed of them at the very far end of the property line earlier in the day. A lone squirrel and a few rabbits were nibbling on the endless supply of lawn dessert, as I envisioned a gangster rat trotting up to the fruit salad causing the rest of the wildlife to run for their lives.

We finally made it to homeownership only to be run out of town by rats.

The town issued guidance on a rat surge, and the advice was as disturbing as the problem. I envisioned the scenes from cattle mutilations on ranches out west occurring in our backyard. When I'm disturbed or upset, I usually relay those problems to Michelle, which helps me but doesn't help her. She is remarkably strong-willed and resolute, but will eventually crack like any healthy yet overwatered tomato.

"Oh good, we have instant mashed potatoes," I told Michelle one evening as she arrived home from work.

Michelle was still taking part in the devil's march, somehow dealing with the shock of my recent diagnosis, doctors' visits, and escalating face-masking policies because of a worldwide pandemic. She kept it together, somehow. "Why?" she asked, looking puzzled at my trivial interest in food inventory when the rest of our world and the one outside our crooked house had gone to shit.

"For the rats."

"They like instant mashed potatoes, too?"

"I guess. We just put that outside in a dish, then pour some water in another dish so that when the rats eat it, they get thirsty, drink the water, and become bloated and die."

"Oh, wow."

The thought of rats overeating and exploding in the yard with Idaho potato mortar in their belly initially made us laugh before contemplating how disturbing that would be and why, exactly, we were paying taxes and a mortgage. The desert seemed better than this; we were never threatened by the cormorants, lizards, or the owl that once scared us when it swooped down to kill a mouse on one of our evening strolls. I considered packing the car and heading west before it turned dark and we were under siege by some unstoppable rodent army.

FALL 2020

SOMETIMES VILLAINS ARE SUBTLE, sleepy, insidious creatures that let their guard down or adopt a gentler strategy to poke fun at your plight. I was finally feeling at ease with the prospect of purchasing our first home, mainly because interest rates had dropped to historic lows and the worldwide pandemic had passed by our lives like the angel of death had to Hebrew-owned blood-stained doorways in biblical Egypt. Spared from pathological contraction or at least distressing symptoms, I was grateful that my mysterious back pain had also subsided. It seemed like a sign from the heavens that homesteading was in our future, even as prices escalated as fast as pandemic death toll numbers and toilet paper on the black market.

The hunt for a residence was far more challenging than finding paper products. Michelle and I were second-guessing any chance of achieving *It's A Wonderful Life* underdog success right as the local bank branch closed down. We wondered whether a plan to head back west to where the buffalo used to roam was perhaps the *better* life plan.

Maybe there's a little gold left in Vulture City we could mine?

The internet can teach you anything, even how to build an affordable, adobe-style house out of mud. The possibility became our unofficial plan B even though we are not architects, don't have a contractor's license, and hate following directions. We continued the house search, shelved plan B, and had our realtor running us to every foreclosure, short sale, and abandoned shack with a decent-sized yard. These properties were usually cheaper than the combined household value of SUVs occupying many neighborhood driveways, even though the initial strategy was to find a low-cost starter home. However, those were all remodeled and painted gray for a premium price, so we expanded the search to include anything qualifying for a mortgage. Turns out the best bargains are beige because until gray is on every wall in every house, gray won't be as despised as beige, sagging drop ceilings, or linoleum.

Maybe we should pack two bags, donate the rest of our belongings, and go live in a cave such as the ones we visited in Walnut Canyon? That might bring us joy, at first.

We were not cheap, per se, just plagued by remnant college loans competing in a severely overpriced market. Bargain hunting the most appalling options with fresh face masks and complimentary sanitizing wipes eroded our confidence. Considering dwellings that were so unlevel and bowed left our befuddled home inspector recommending a structural engineer. I suspect he might have actually thought we needed counseling.

Powder post beetle damage? Check.

Rot? Check.

Sill beam missing? Check.

Termites, carpenter ants, squirrels? Check.

Haunted? Check. Poor decision? Check.

"Do we write the inspector a check?" I asked Michelle. "Or pay with a card or cash?"

After paying for a critical review of a broken home that was affordable but hopelessly unrepairable, we asked ourselves during an endless series of stress walks if we should just resort to hobo Boho van life and admit defeat? I was nothing more than an amateur chess player, but the house search was disheartening, and the market seemed to say checkmate. Finding a house was as tricky as encountering a Boston Market near Boston, which is also as perplexing as ironic.

BOSTON'S DROWNING in some serious money, and most outsiders can't waltz in for the experience as if it's a theme park. Maybe the roaring '20s never left, or the IRS never showed up in the first place? I'm convinced even the football players and part-time-fintech-hidden-wealth-"working"-from-home people have Gatsby beat. He'd probably feel uncomfortable and duck out before even uttering a single *"old sport"* after a local holiday party or weekend Cape house invitation. The clever swindler would have to reinvent his blue blood scamming operations and market with a sexy app that has some blue-chip facade. Despite my best efforts, I've got nothing on even Gatsby's poor bond sales agent neighbor, and I've even dabbled in bonds despite the Fed's manipulation and Michelle's reservations.

I think I need to find a place like Portland before it was trending, but with the coffee obsession of somewhere like Seattle minus the humidity or depression, and something as unrestricted as Texas without the superiority complex or draw—oh, that's right, Arizona! It's a shame Californian migration is driving up home prices in the Copper State. However, land parcels in Arizona are still more affordable than what people pay for dirt to be delivered for their new lawn project in most Boston suburbs. Since Arizona barely taxes it, maybe a camper hitched up to the cheating diesel wagon and a bottled-water rural delivery plan is the beautiful life hack answer to our problems?

I just have to pack all our possessions into a car, which may take some time and probably requires a permit. Really, though, I should prioritize: place some bets on a football team, sell some inflated stocks with the app named after Prince John's nemesis, and go skiing. Maybe round up any cash and copper we have, exchange it for crypto, and figure out how to cancel streaming services. That's all a lot of work, though, so if I was as affable as most suburban Bostonians, I would hire someone to manage all that for me while I focused on a new health trend or vacation to prelude any big life changes. Unfortunately, we still have to drink coffee at home, cook chicken in a Crock-Pot, and opt out of the milk delivery, so I can't afford to subcontract.

Instead, I'll just sip a homemade brew from a mismatched, chipped coffee mug, browse the Go Fund Me pages, and never set one up for myself because the other stories always seem sadder and somehow worse. I guess I'll forfeit charity and suppress temporary unemployment-induced anxiety, opting to stare at the plaster cracks competing with flaking lead paint chips, and dream of a more perfect life in the desert. All while attempting to write a clever, therapeutic memoir set in the pandemic-plagued 2020s from an understuffed mail-order couch that is less comfortable than an old sport coupe seat that's slowly being disassembled by mice in a New England barn.

Supposedly, determination and hard work pay off, and after a few months of intense searching, the real gem appeared closer to Providence than Boston. It was the first house to be inhabited primarily by humans, so it seemed promising. The price was higher than what we had considered spending, the upside being its enviable proximity to work and a desirable location. That meant I didn't need the rally car anymore, so I gleefully sold it, paying off one of the many remaining student loans since I still believed I could take care of all my problems on my own. The new location meant we could walk to our jobs, in a pinch, and the planned dispensary the town had approved but since retracted. The game was finally tilting in our favor, because maybe the "house" has to let you win sometimes or the villains were taking an extended coffee nap. We brushed aside the apparent history of neglect and outdatedness, wholeheartedly embracing the idea of regaining our independence. Michelle and I were finally on track to enjoying "the good life" typified in all those black-and-white films characterized by homemade pies resting on the windowsill, picket fences, and escrow.

It was typical and old, with a New England Cape-style architecture converted to be more spacious. Despite the changes throughout time, it retained its character, crookedness, and probable ghosts. The charming white-and-black-trimmed house that the realtor decided to call a "colonial" was on a quiet historic street, lined with sidewalks with glossy stone curbs and mature shade trees. If the neighbors were mature, they had kids and dogs that had the decency *not* to do their business on your front lawn, and everybody rolled the trash barrel back up their driveways promptly after the truck rolled down the street.

Our arrival seemed too good to be true.

The neighborhood was strictly working-class, and everyone seemed to value their quarter-acre slice of the American dream, mowing their lawns on weekend mornings and jumping into the above-ground pools they assembled themselves or with helpful neighbors. Nearly everyone had a functional firepit. When the smoke predictably curled above all the fenced-in yards on a calm summer night, the smell of hard-earned success seemed burned into the identity of the street. It captured the soul-stirring feeling you get when the fireworks display is over on the Fourth of July, as that looming smoke cloud slowly drifts away. The weekend cookouts and lawn-chair circles invoked an overwhelming sense of accomplishment, and New England life finally seemed refreshing.

The hedge fund guys were definitely not making their bets here, and the trust fund pretentiousness hanging over Boston was refreshingly absent.

YOU COULD SAY the house had an 1800s rustic charm or was remarkably dated. Despite the oversize windows, the lighting was unexpectedly dim, characterized by a single low-watt bulb that descended from the spider web fractured ceiling, not in the middle of the kitchen or centered with anything except where your head was when walking to the fridge. The windows that *did* open that were not painted shut invited the prevailing winds to air out the posts and beams and fieldstone foundation. That capability was important because there was no central AC and the only ceiling fan was outside with sagging blades in an enclosed porch which leaned away from the original home, suggesting it was trying to divorce it after years of being forcibly attached. Although it had its faults, drawbacks, and knob-and-tube wiring, the sturdy old girl felt as reliable as an ancient ship having weathered many storms. It made up for its deficiencies in spirit, and that seemed good enough for us.

Michelle and I bought a six-pack and sat on the bare, rough floor littered with remnant carpet staples in what we were calling the "dining room" even though it was actually the makeshift workshop of the new house we were tearing apart. There were many reasons to celebrate. It was 2020, and a new decade had begun. It was also the year we entered *our* next decade, the 30s. We finally had a house for the first time and had survived COVID. A new chapter commenced, and we toasted the occasion under the glow of the dim floor lamp in an otherwise empty room. As we raised a bottle, the words were as valid as the level resting on our dishonest floor, and I will never forget them: "I sure as hell hope our 30s are better than our 20s. That would be nice."

THE BEGINNING of October marked our arrival and subsequent secret renovation, since inspections and permits are a real pain in the ass. We began by stripping the carpets, revealing tired wood plank floors that needed more sanding than initially assessed, and scrubbing the included appliances that were dirtier than organic produce. Soon we moved on to more significant projects like patching old plaster appearing as delicate in some spots as pudding. Walls needed painting, doors needed adjusting, and the cellar needed a thorough cleaning, but probably more of a priest's blessing than anything else. I remember tearing multiple layers of the old vinyl floor out, worrying I would also tear some muscle or ligament. However, much to my surprise and relief, I was spared any physical affliction during our best reenactment of *The Money Pit*. But that was before my brother showed up on the scene as confident as a contractor, minus the credentials.

The reinforcements arrived after an invitation that may have resembled a panic call with the promise of free food and boxes of coffee on tap, and I recall buying some cigarettes for my brother. *Because what else does a good older sibling do when he needs some help?* Pretty soon, the Camaro with all tint and no exhaust screeched to a halt in front of the house, my brother apprehensively approaching the *This Old House*–style project, minus the budget, crew, and very few power tools. The tour began with an assessment in the kitchen and ended with extensive contemplation in the cellar, where a rotted window was caving in.

"DAMN, THERE ARE a lot of pallets down here."

"I know, EJ. I wonder why?"

"At least it looks dry, though. That's good."

"Yeah, maybe it gets a little damp sometimes. I don't know."

"Looks like they used to have a sump pump. Huh, the pit is filled with dirt, though. The pump is clogged with sand."

"Guess that's a good sign, bro. It must be rare that it gets damp. Probably just a little puddle where that rotted window is letting the rain in."

We inspected the frame around the window as my brother picked up the fragile remnant resting unattached on the sill. He held it up in the air, and it turned to powder.

"Yeah, we need to fix that. But first, I need a smoke break."

I agreed, and we should have strictly repaired the window, but that would be too easy, so we pissed off the ghosts instead. An old cane was resting, nearly hidden, on the concrete form near the top of the foundation, next to the propped-open rotted window. We noticed it sitting among some rusty hinges that someone must've been collecting a few decades ago. They were ancient, and the cane looked older than both our ages combined.

"What the hell is that?" I asked.

"Oh damn, a cane."

"What do we do with it? Put it back like the cross over the washer?"

Nicotine cravings were distracting my brother, he had a lapse of judgment, or sometimes just likes to tempt fate. *Maybe that is why he smokes so much, drives so fast, and sets off fireworks despite neighborly complaints?* I don't know why his advice sometimes seems appropriate, but I didn't feel compelled to object.

"Nah, I say we snap it to let the spirit out. That way, it won't haunt the house."

I stared at the wooden cane, a little worried, and shrugged. "Sure, bro, snap it."

EJ broke the cane over his knee with a slight laugh and little effort, as if it was a tree branch going to be discarded into the firepit. He tossed it into a contractor trash bag we hauled out of the cellar with a bunch of other debris the previous inhabitants had left behind. I was a little worried but my brother casually strolled outside for a smoke, either a naive kid or professional ghost hunter.

I wish the previous homeowners had taken the cane, or we hadn't disturbed it. Little did I know the object was possessed or cursed and that my spine would snap not even a year later. We probably committed a brazen haunted-house sin, releasing some unstable villain with a lame leg who thought it was funny to flood the bone-dry cellar and smoke something invisible that activated the smoke detector. My mom believes *something* lives down there, and when she visits, bids "Mister Cane" farewell when doing laundry. I laugh at the preposterous joke until I'm alone in the house. That's when my macho facade crumbles and I double-check the lock on the cellar door, crank up some music on the Wi-Fi speaker, and blame unexplainable noises on neighborhood dogs.

That usually helps, until the internet suddenly goes out for no known reason.

Our modernization exercise was a deliberate and quick success. Everything brightened up after applying a different palette of paints, and actual working light bulbs transformed the ancient enterprise into something resembling a "real" home that was really ours. We had saved for years to get to this point, and it was a great feeling to begin the next chapter of our lives with measurable square footage and a driveway for a future fleet of exciting road-trip-inspiring jalopies. I reminded Michelle again as we reflected on all the remaining problems, "At least we have each other, especially our health."

BACK WHEN CHOCOLATE bars were not as thin and still wrapped in paper, I was frustratingly thin, studying the local newspaper that landed somewhere in the front rhododendron bush every morning. I was probably too young to read about stocks and bonds, but inexperience did not deter me to do better than my parents. I enjoyed researching and reading well-written articles about investing, circling with a pen local company tickers and guessing how much I'd make if I had skin in the game. Despite all the knowledge and drive at a young age, I ignored my better judgment and racked up more student loans than probably all the debts my parents accumulated over their entire lives. That's why I am typing this document on a table with a shim under the leg in a crooked house at 31 fucking years old that Michelle and I could barely afford.

I'm not complaining; unwise past decisions are the least of my problems. Besides, the bizarre environmental curiosities of an old "sinking ship-esque" house does provide some comedic relief. It's a beautiful structure with a few solid bones—except where the plaster is paper-thin and newspapers are pasted to the walls lining the cellar stairs, supposedly for insulation. *That* decorating choice was ugly as fuck, for sure, but I'm not judging. There's nothing a little elbow grease and five hundred coats of primer and gray paint can't hide. Except, of course, where the mice made a mess tunneling under the foundation and the bees bored into the siding. It seems remarkable, though, that we have seen no mice *inside*, but that might be because an owl or—as Michelle speculates on some evenings—"roof rats" visit the attic.

The dwelling possessed more character than the combined cast of *Caddyshack*. I only hoped gopher-rat hybrids, evil cane-wielding ghosts, or yet another villain did not possess it. Paint the trim, patch the walls, and figure out what a light switch that does nothing is for. The chores and surprise repairs were endless, but I didn't mind keeping busy because being alive and overburdened has always seemed better than being bored and dead. *The same policy seems even more applicable now. I don't want to be idly stewing in a chair dwelling on spinal villains trying to kill me as a roof rat battles an owl, recreating some scene from* Harry Potter.

Honestly, though, I didn't know I signed up for this. I thought I was buying an old jalopy of a house that needed a little time, love, and care like the TV shows like to advertise. Just slap on the gray paint, shiplap the walls, and everything turns out fantastic. Instead, I'm the unlicensed captain of a sinking, wooden boat that creaks when the winds pick up and takes on water when the groundwater rises. The lights flicker if the window AC or dehumidifier is running, and the microwave and coffee maker can't be used at the same time. I kind of miss the days when the evolution of a candy bar was my biggest dilemma or when local stocks tanked my hypothetical portfolio.

EVERYTHING WAS GOING WELL until after a rainy week around Thanksgiving. The cellar was damp and overnight became a swimming pool the size of Lake Powell with no clear boundaries. The "deep end" was suspiciously where we snapped the cane.

"Sweetie, we don't have a permit for a swimming pool in the cellar. We need a shovel, sump pump, and a hole saw attachment for the drill."

We shopped for the items with the urgency of a Black Friday sale, running back to the deluge in the tallest boots we owned, which seemed adequate during Maine snow adventures but were not so helpful when excavating a sump pump pit in a rising lake. I was convinced shoveling wet and heavy mud would flare up my recovered back, but much to my surprise, I was perfectly fine. I watched plenty of documentary dramas showing the gold miners searching for precious metals, experiencing one calamity after another, so I expected the worst scenario possible. I smashed my boot on the shovel repeatedly in a race to save the house, or at least our furniture, from floating away. Luckily, when we plugged in the pump and the cellar drained like an oversize bathtub, it stayed drained, and I felt terrific.

Huh, I guess the shoveling in my recent past was different. Maybe the cellar wasn't as haunted as the previous residence? Thank God we left that cross above the washing machine and didn't have to inherit a cursed cat.

The following five months were similarly fantastic. I drank a lot of drive-through coffee in a box with a spout, teetered on a makeshift sawhorse to fuel my renovation surge, and dealt with the coinciding parcel surge that makes all postal employees skeptical of Santa's unrealistic Christmas quota. I brewed green tea most nights because flavonoids prevent inflammation and the aura of the tea kettle turned out to be the warmest part of a drafty, old, uninsulated New England house. I soon became content and foolishly thought the new home was a fortress sparing me from the wrath of all former villains. *Maybe they couldn't find me at the new residence since I committed a cardinal postal sin and refused to change my address? What luck!*

INTERMISSION II:
A POEM

I WOULDN'T CONSIDER myself a talented pianist, just an aggravated novice who sits at a keyboard once in a while to butcher classical music. That's not to say with sufficient effort and Arabica bean juice, I can't rattle off some Mozart. Likewise, I couldn't become a butcher with adequate training because I like blood less than playing arpeggios and music theory. The hospital reminded me of these limitations every day. I cringed at the daily morning blood test, nervously glancing over at the spinal fluid on the pole, which turned crimson whenever I moved too much or became nervous. I'd rather have someone force me to practice scales and inaptly recite the circle of fifths. These days I was reciting to doctors and nurses how I felt on the pain scale, which lingered closer to 10 than 1, maybe fluctuating between 5 and 7.

The pain hadn't stopped me from writing, just as sarcasm didn't deter me from once penning three lines of poetry. Michelle was digging through a growing mountain of insurance statements and medical files when she found the poem suspiciously resembling a haiku I had penned as a joke. I had written it right before most villains consumed my existence. Although brief, I now realize how the simplest expressions convey what we want or experience better than anything else, which must be why emojis or certain hand gestures exist. If I could reduce this entire French memory story to three lines, I cannot think of a more appropriate substitute than this rediscovered prose:

Brew me a dark roast
New England is a cold rugged place
I'm moving to the desert

MY CURRENT DIAGNOSIS has only reinforced the authenticity of this assessment; perhaps I could play some street piano for cold-brew-obsessed Scottsdale tourists. Or go rouge and flee to Snowflake, since Mormons and marijuana may collectively deter villains, or maybe Page, which gives the Grand Canyon a run for its money and is guaranteed to confuse any villain's cellphone clock with perpetual time zone tricks.

VILLAIN NUMBER 11: THE MAGICAL JUICE

APRIL 2021

THE TWO-FOOT-TALL "CEDAR" was turning a lifeless pale brown, having lived in the same clay pot for a few years, obviously unhappy with confined root space and overwatered soil. It sat outside our new house near a downspout, ready to be planted when the ground thawed. I was worried it might be dead because it looked dead.

The weekend before Memorial Day, I was shoveling some rocks in the yard—carefully, to not "fuck up again" like the cat grave villain made clear almost two years prior. I desperately wanted to plant the cedar tree after moving some rocks, since my wife had saved it, transferring the tree to our new residence in the back of her station wagon. I was skeptical it could be saved, but it didn't matter—I was going to plant it, finally, in our very own yard. The dream was coming true, and the future seemed better. The weather was warmer and life seemed a little easier for once.

As it turns out, that was strictly a mirage, a villainous concocted illusion disguised as a reprieve, obscuring a cruel reality.

I didn't get to plant the tree. Overnight, my back was worse than it ever had been. My one last-ditch effort to remedy the issue began with a subscription to physical therapy that only made everything worse. It was hell. I could barely walk, stand, sit, or recline and probably looked as healthy as our nearly dead cedar. *I wanted to plant the pathetic thing, I swear, but I couldn't even move without lightning shooting through my spine.*

THE STRAW that broke the camel's back must have contained osmium, or maybe the camel was unusually frail. I sure as hell wasn't doing the camel pose or any of the other pretzel poses the flexible therapists wanted me to perform. I was in near-constant pain, starting to believe I was as frail as a strand of uncooked angel hair pasta or my bones resembled straw, minus the osmium. Desperation was setting in, and the enrollment in the health insurance–sponsored torture sessions was the last straw before the aliens reared their ugly heads on a black-and-white photo of my spine.

Undeterred by my reservations, I mustered enough courage to enroll in physical therapy, even though I had heard many mixed reviews about it over the years. Without admitting my skepticism, I began the program with an open mind since mixed-review movies, musical albums, and debut memoirs often turn out to be good.

It began with an assessment, assigned stretches I already was familiar with, and a maintenance plan eerily similar to the chiro-practor's. However, it was different because "we ultimately don't want you to come back for your back," they informed me. I applauded the anti-dealership, anti-crack and bone popping chiropractic agenda since it promised long-term solutions I could manage independently, hopefully providing permanent relief. The first recommendation, though, caused me to research "gambler's conceit" and consider running for the exit, not that I could even run anymore.

The first recommendation was the cherry juice plan.

THIS WASN'T the first time someone had introduced me to the concept of health. Michelle and I made drastic dietary changes post-college. We became committed to preempting the disparate health problems various aged family members had experienced over the years. Nursing homes, rehab, and endless drug subscriptions seemed like a horrible ending to our pretty good beginning, and we wanted to avoid those outcomes if possible. Even after moving back in with Michelle's family, who was hell-bent on replicating the *Sopranos* diet, we drew a line in the sand, planted a garden, and staged a coup d'état of the cabinets and fridge. We purged the colorful bowls brimming with leftover white pasta, white rice, and white potatoes. We stocked whole-some groceries and produce that would make any "blue zone" devotee, Seventh-day Adventist, or vegan proud. My in-laws, however, were traditional Italian-Irish-American-blooded consumers of everything developed in cans, boxes, and bottles by post–World War II chemical engineering industrialists. They were devastated when we attempted to impose a Mediterranean diet.

I remember my sugar-addicted father-in-law trying to bribe me with actual cash to buy the "naughty food" or something "a little sweet," but we never gave in. They were now forced to buy that stuff and find a place to store it on their own or convert. Michelle and I were busy baptizing the virtual junk food ware-house with natural nutrition to everyone's benefit. There were no more snacks made of chemicals, refined grains, or toxic bever-ages loaded up with sugars and colors resembling antifreeze. We thought we were on the right track, avoiding the crap, hoping the whole foods and virgin olive oils would save us from the pharmaceutical dependence.

The commercials often persuade us to "eat the greasy burger and take a pill because your heart isn't happy" or "sign up for these treatments because all the pixie stick sugar is rotting your gut." Interestingly, some people "detox" or "cleanse" and record their trials and tribulations on video and blog posts, but get depressed when the views stop coming in. The drug companies have a solution, of course: "Take this sedative when you're depressed from quitting all the foods and sodas that are addictive and deadly. If the pill gives you an adverse side effect, here's another pill to help with all that." The cycle is as endless as creative.

Self-deprivation and reckless avoidance, though, might not be worth it. Occasionally I would sneak a coffee roll, not that my wife cared or was a health saint herself. She'd eat all the ice cream after a tough day power-marching the mail around in spite of severe dairy intolerance. During my hospital adventure, I abandoned most of my nutritional ideals. I committed many culinary crimes, like ordering chocolate pudding with every meal or eating French toast for breakfast *and* dinner. However, we ate better than the average American, and the plan seemed destined to protect us from future complications.

Now I'm not so sure.

The suggestion to "inhale this potent oil," "take this supplement," "stop dairy," or "not be so tense" when you walk around in pain seemed like advice from people who either didn't have any real issues or enjoyed pyramid scheme paychecks. Suppose a supplement, vitamin, or essential oil in a bottle prescribed by someone with the credentials of Dr Pepper could solve my current problems better than the collective medical wisdom of Boston. In that case, I would raid my retirement account and buy all of it, or at least the preferred shares of stock in those companies.

. . .

THE BEST HEALING juice is squeezed from a "100 percent cherry," which is the tart, bitter, unsweetened kind with the viscosity of used motor oil with a reddish tint. It smells as pungent as cough syrup and tastes as good as canned beets. The juice stains everything it touches like blood, and it might be just as expensive, but unfortunately, it's not covered by insurance. Its value is invaluable since it may, in some people, rival the benefits of ibuprofen, minus the adverse side effects. Michelle and I sought to make a quest out of sampling the different brands from different local sources so that I might finally cure my stubborn inflammation.

You can consult the internet experts and find many mixing recipes to improve the odds of successfully consuming the magical juice. I tried them all, including my therapist's recommendation to pull out a tablespoon and down the natural cureall every night before bed like a shot of whiskey. Although the placebo effect is remarkably potent, I wish it worked because the advertised healing nutrients and compounds found in the magical juice were not. I tried to embrace its pungent bitterness and the stained butcher-block countertop's blood-colored crop circles with enthusiasm and optimism. After a few weeks of use, it became clear the potion was a scam.

The only apparent effect was of the laxative kind, which I had no use for. I already drank coffee, and for the first time in my life I decided *I would prefer to drink box wine.*

Scams always target the elderly in the mail, by landline phone, and on cable TV. Perhaps the silver-haired Social Security crowd outnumbered me at most physical therapy sessions. They probably also need the most help in the "staying regular" department of their lives, so some scams are probably helpful to certain people. I'm sure for someone physical therapy is a valid path toward healing. The problem was it wasn't helping my condition because, like all previous attempts to solve my dilemma, no one knew what my symptoms meant.

The advice addressed every conceivable culprit:

- Strengthen the muscles around where it hurts.
- Stretch the muscles on both sides equally. Every day. Twice a day.
- Show up here twice a week.
- Sleep with four or five pillows.
- Try a different therapist.
- Drink more magical juice. And water. And supplements.
- Try expensive shoes.
- Maybe take a vacation.

I heard it all, and none of the recommendations or expressed positivity mattered. They were purely speculative solutions trying to solve my unknown problems, as valuable as getting an ill-advised stock tip to buy cruise ship and amusement park companies before a worldwide pandemic. It's not their fault they didn't know why the cat-cow pose wasn't helping or that cable TV sages and stockbroker algorithms can't predict the future.

A nice Californian merlot would be much more approach-able, and about the exact cost of a physical therapy copay. However, superb wine isn't cheap, and cheap wine produces a predictable splitting headache. I abstained from the swill my family calls "vino" because no amount of alcohol would dull the radiating, scorpion-stinging terror that vanished and reappeared as unpredictably as a stoned blind cat ghost-tripping on catmint down uneven stairs. I know because I tried some moderate drinking experiments (minus the catmint) during an *Outlander* binge marathon. If you never have, you probably shouldn't start now. Unless there are villains at your door trying to pick the locks with an ax or broadsword or an MRI reveals being as fucked as Claire is every goddamn second of her life.

Slowly sipping some top-shelf scotch (whose name I can't pronounce but smells like peat) whenever the time-traveling duo made a terrible decision provided unnoticeable relief and a regrettable hangover, despite my alleged 10 percent Scottish heritage.

This discovery was annoying because every Western I grew up watching while clutching a bowl of pasta depicted someone clutching a bottle of something alcoholic to numb their trauma. I soon realized television had been nothing more than a scam at this point in my life because the booze wasn't working. Beers, wines, and some barrel-aged spirits were as useless as the cherry juices. This was as worrisome as the ibuprofen regimen that was also not helping. Desperate measures were futile, and another X-ray showed absolutely not a single problem with my spine. I wasn't sure how I could always lift wrong, walk wrong, or not stretch or strengthen the right muscles, and I kept squinting at the adverse side effects on the bottles of pain pills, which no doctors seemed to be worried about. I contemplated booking a flight to Scotland and finding the mystical stoned fairies. With Michelle, of course. Maybe my pagan ancestors could help?

THE STRETCHING, MASSAGING, CELEBRITY-ENDORSED "CUPPING," and juice regimen were ineffective, as multiple sessions became weeks of copays, frustration, and increased discomfort. Strengthening and releasing tight, farfalle-knotted muscles only aggravated my back, leg, side, hip, and groin, preventing me from sleeping, going to work, or driving Michelle's three-pedal car. The pain grew to new heights, ultimately forcing me to despise the magical fruity elixir some New England Wiccans who were infiltrating physical therapy establishments have cursed. I didn't even have a chance. I followed the rules and sought help, but was lured into a scam by shape-shifter alien therapists, foolishly drinking the villainous juice of the black cherry.

I reported these findings to my doctor, and she recommended I end the plan and abandon yet another dark horse, much to my relief. Since this was such an unexpected and undesirable result, we agreed on seeking the advice of an MRI. That's when I discovered my real villain.

VILLAIN NUMBER 12: THE ALIEN INVASION

MAY 2021

CASINOS ARE LOUD AND DARK, don't have windows or clocks, and you'll be out of a lot of money when you enter one —*identical to an MRI*. I prayed when the humming and scanning stopped, and my eyes opened, that there wouldn't be a $50 bill in my pocket and I wouldn't be dead. If my real villain is an alien who lives in my spine, I wouldn't be surprised. However, I'm pretty confident the odds of being abducted by aliens seem pretty high, whereas having a diagnosis as rare as I do is significantly lower. It's statistically something ridiculously frustrating and perplexing, like maybe you'd get hit by lightning during an Arizona monsoon *and* win the lottery on the same day. Or maybe less. No one knows. All I knew was it felt like time was running out, as Matt Bellamy sang, and I didn't want to wind up dead before I had even mastered part I of "Exogenesis: Symphony" on our dusty piano.

I WAS DRINKING a therapeutic iced coffee as Michelle drove us back from the local hospital, transferring my weight from one side of the seat to another, wondering what the outcome of the radiological test would be. I stretched my legs out because they were tight, shoving a borrowed couch pillow behind my back. The pain of my hip, sciatica, or whatever was severely irritated was magnified any time we drove over a bump in the road. Sitting in the car had become nearly impossible the two weeks leading up to this MRI. I blamed it entirely on the physical therapy. It was a strenuous routine, and now my mobility was suffering. I told my boss I needed a week off to let the inflammation "cool down." The medication wasn't even taking the edge off anymore.

The test took over an hour, which seemed like a long time to lie flat on your back without moving while dealing with pinched nerves. I'd imagined this was what it was like to lie in a coffin when buried alive, but without the radio station crackling in the headphones the hospital staff had graciously provided. *It probably was going to confirm the previous guesses about unaligned joints or nerves being pinched*, I remember convincing myself repeatedly. My primary doctor reminded me that would mean a recommendation for "more physical therapy." Wincing at the suggestion, I shifted uncomfortably on the tissue paper–lined doctor's office table, instantly regretting my decision to finally get an MRI.

Convinced the likelihood of any *other* outcome wasn't possible, I settled into a chair when we arrived at home and started reading a book my mom had sent me about political conspiracies and UFO pilots running the Pentagon. It was distracting me from the unknown, my villains, and the ibuprofen that was wearing off, which was nice.

Eventually, the phone rang. It was the primary doctor. She sounded as if she had had a few energy drinks. "You'll be seeing a specialist tomorrow. At the latest."

"OK," I replied.

A brief pause.

"OK?" she asked.

"Yes," I answered, feeling a little sick.

"There's a mass. A mass in your spine."

Everything was suddenly not OK, but I think I said "OK" anyway.

I stopped sipping my iced coffee, never returned to the conspiracy book, and was speechless after thanking her for an unexpected dagger in the gut.

My blank face was as expressionless and pale as a flyleaf. I tried not to panic.

I told Michelle, and we both panicked together.

Time seemed to stop.

But my mind was racing.

I was spiraling out of control in a stalled Cessna that had its wings chopped off at 20,000 feet by Tic Tac alien spaceships that didn't want to share airspace.

That's just a nightmare I get if I eat a spicy burrito and fall asleep watching conspiracy TV shows. The sinking feeling seizing your stomach when a roller coaster or plane pitches violently is what hit me when I put the phone down.

I sat down, but it wouldn't go away.

I couldn't believe this horrific revelation.

No wonder the heating pad didn't help or the ice, Advil, stretching, car seats, clutches, mattresses, the placebo effect, expensive juices, positive thoughts, walking, resting, vacations, and holy fucking hell in a handbasket delivered by the devil himself. This was bad news.

The doctors dropped the grenade that was my diagnosis in my lap but the villains may as well have tossed a few sticks of dynamite on our leaky roof. I stared at the textured wall and the clock ticking louder than it ever had before, relieved to have identified the truth of my pain but terrified the reality was much worse than I ever imagined. It was the biggest shock of our lives, and I was sure someone had handed me a death sentence. I consulted Doctor Google, convinced "mass" meant the end. *"The devil's march is now over."*

MAYBE BEING responsible doesn't pay off? At least in this life. Honesty, integrity, industriousness, and paying the bills on time resulted in a backstabbing kick in the teeth despite facing our challenges head-on. I don't blame God, though, because he must be busy dealing with the pandemic and rogue Tic Tac alien spacecraft who probably want to kill us all, like in War of the Worlds, trying to counter politicians who are busy tweeting instead of preventing World War III. My prayers must've been sitting under a stack of those of a million others, and I do not know what the cloud storage capacity or delivery methods are like up there. If Silicon Valley tech conglomerates are running it, that would explain a lot.

Maybe my guardian angel was overwhelmed by all the other villains, missing the one inflicting the most damage, or the prayer network doesn't have a good firewall?

I don't know why this is happening, but I do know people often say "everything happens for a reason." I think most people who dish out canned wisdom are selfish pricks whose most significant challenge is figuring out what sports jersey they're going to buy. Although I don't want to be bitter, everything tastes as sour as a lime when encountering the vain, self-absorbed nonsense of what most people post or say. I can only pray that I won't end up like Job because I'm not competitive and I don't care about winning challenges. Unless it's a guacamole challenge. Then I'd probably kick ass and win.

Perhaps my lifelong prayer for good health was hacked by Russia? Just kidding. China? Just kidding. North Korea? Just kidding. I don't want to fuel another world war. It was probably some disgruntled hero Gen Z kids burned out from two years of virtual academics, hell-bent on unleashing the notorious "Gh0st RAT" because this new century is looking as worrisome as the beginning of the last one. Might as well wreak havoc if other countries do it all the time and the aliens are landing soon anyway. Realistically, though, maybe it's Lucifer's hacking army, which is perhaps staffed by the scammed souls of disgruntled delivery employees who were promised a half-acre lot, a new house on Mars, and a crypto pension that was supposed to be superior to post office benefits.

THE BLACK-AND-WHITE IMAGERY was remarkably familiar, and the word *irony* took on a new meaning. Was there any difference between an MRI and a Department of Defense satellite image? With varying levels of confidence, the scene is interpreted. Hopefully, the interpreter was right, or I would be cut open and nuked by radiation or a foreign enemy would receive a similar fate. As I popped more ibuprofen and braced for every bump on the cratered road as Michelle drove us to the city, this repeated reflection circulated in my mind.

In less than 24 hours after the fateful phone call, we were arriving in Boston to meet with a neurosurgeon, as my primary doctor had promised. When he confirmed what "mass" meant, he seemed as confident as Dr. House, minus the limp and cane, that they could remove it, and I should not be consuming magical juices if I didn't like the taste. The doctor followed this observation by dropping the real bombshell. He announced that this "bad luck" was not because of diet, genetics, cigarettes, drinking, snowmobiling, evil thoughts, or even junk mail. It was down to two simple words defining why I was screwed: bad luck. *Fuck.*

My real villain was the shape of a sausage, relatively large and pressing on all the nerves that all the other villains seemed to pinch. What an elusive son of a bitch. The lab confirmed the alien's name post-surgery, and it is a mouthful: *myxopapillary ependymoma.* Again, I was highly encouraged "not to Google it," but I felt sick and tried not to scream when I eventually did.

Some doctors call it benign; others call it *slow spinal cord cancer*.

They all call it a disease and really bad luck.

NERVE PAIN IS an exclusive experience like Alienware was before Dell bought them out. The magical juice's effects were supposed to be cumulative, although the experience of drinking the cherry sludge wasn't even desirable despite the cult following. Naproxen gave me an immediate reaction. It was hell. I thought I might die before I paid off my student loans, the mortgage, Michelle got a poison ivy tattoo, or I mastered "The Minute Waltz" on the piano that was becoming more of a temporary shelf for broken laptop computers because new technology is cheap crap. *Maybe Michelle is as strong as a superhero villain?*

I was anxiously waiting for my scheduled surgery and "taking it easy" for a stressful two weeks. Even the transition from sitting to standing was excruciating, as a radiating, electrical tinge would stab me near the tailbone and hip. With little to no success with ibuprofen, I tried the giant bottle of naproxen Michelle picked up at the pharmacy. It looked as oversized as a tallboy, containing a few hundred pills. I took a single, bloated Tic Tac pill before bed. About an hour later, I woke up and thought something was electrocuting my legs as I groggily cursed the house's old wiring.

My eyes were heavy and aching.

My forehead was throbbing.

I definitely had a migraine.

Is space dementia real? If it is, then this might be it.

A mild dose of profanity can be refreshing and appropriate under certain circumstances. However, when you're contemplating a health crisis, staring down death's dark corridor, and have a headache rivaling the Havana syndrome, the f-word just doesn't cut it. Cursing prompted by such duress can become an unstoppable torrent of dictionary pillaging, and that is precisely what I did because everything was going to shit.

I limped out of the bedroom and into the kitchen to find the bottle of medication, squinting to read the side effects. In the back of my mind, I was worried the tumor was growing and about to kill me right before the operation, because that would be my kind of luck, wouldn't it? After an hour or two of pacing, drinking a ton of fluids, and taking a shower, the effects wore off. I guess that's what a drug overdose feels like. It sucks. Eventually, I fell back asleep, but predictably not for very long.

OVER TWO YEARS leading up to this diagnosis, I had become accustomed to decreasing sleep quality and minimal dreaming. I would toss and turn in bed and perform a few tornado spins as if I was skateboarding, even though I never skateboarded, finding no comfortable position. I would stretch, eventually give up on sleeping, and wander around downstairs where I would drink more green tea, watch late-night TV, and maybe stretch some more until exhaustion would kick in and knock me out for a while. But it never lasted long enough to reach REM, and it should have caused me more concern. I couldn't differentiate nerve pain from muscle pain, and I'm pretty convinced I have a high tolerance for pain to begin with. Apparently, a hallmark tumor symptom is a pain that wakes you up and keeps you from getting any real, deep sleep.

I know what that's like when even "Santa smut" and alien theorists spinning their conspiracies at 2 a.m. wasn't dull enough to knock me out.

RETURN FROM THE HOSPITAL IN BOSTON

THE BITTERSWEET BOMBSHELL

LATE JUNE 2021

WE CONNECTED via a computer through some hospital "portal" to virtually meet with the referred medical experts to outline a strategy for the treatment my diagnosis required. I was worried the plan would be scarier than my recent surgery, which was itself a shock, and my back was still sore. The stitches remained intact, and they itched more than the mosquitoes that once swarmed my body during a summer cat burial.

I like my steak rare, but not a diagnosis. Nonetheless, that's precisely what it was. The doctor's 1.5-hour-long explanation proved as indolent as the growth of my tumors. It was a rare type in a rare location that was rarely seen. However, since all stories have silver linings, mine was that my brain seemed to have escaped the alien invasion. *For now, anyway.*

Hopefully forever.

The other side of the undesirable condition was it was never going away, and there were many more where it originated. These cells were visible specks throughout my spinal canal, happily "seeding." I envisioned aliens that looked like the Red

Baron flying open-cockpit biplanes, crop spraying newly seeded fields in my spine. It was unsettling.

The experts see very few cases, so they have produced few studies. Most doctors have assured me, though, *I* was in the driver's seat. They would support *my* decision.

How comforting and self-powering. Now I know how passengers in driverless cars will feel when the electronics go haywire—helpless.

I was far from reassured or comforted leading up to this chaotic experience. It seemed like I had somehow traded places with an innocent inmate on death row, aware of my fate yet unaware of when the switch was going to be flipped, presumably because the appeals court kept things stalling or the court documents kept getting lost in the mail because the regular carrier was out on extended sick leave. After all, a tumor may have been trying to kill him. Or, perhaps I embodied that recurring sleazy Wild West villain who always shows up in the movies, saved by a poncho'd benefactor at the last second.

How long will my benefactor keep saving me? Hopefully, it's longer than Michelle's interest in a poncho draped over an extra dining room chair.

My recently acquainted neurosurgeon, whose opinion I highly regard, suggested the best thing might be *nothing*. For now, anyway. Watch it every few months with periodic MRIs and go from there. Live life one day at a time, with no real restrictions, except for skateboarding.

"Don't do that," I was advised. "Twisting could be bad."

Otherwise, don't mess with something that isn't completely broken because it became apparent radiation was worse than a sunburn and perhaps only as helpful as sun lotion while sunbathing near a volcano. It is also the only inevitable option, and it sucks much more than the reruns on antenna TV. Eventually, I will need it, but there are risks and no guarantees it will work long term because this alien son of a bitch that was so fucking rare likes to reappear for an uninvited encore. The drug companies were too busy developing vaccines for world pandemics, diabetes, acne, and common cancers.

Maybe my future would not be as problematic as the one giant alien they already removed?

No one knows except God and perhaps the other aliens living in my spine.

There's nothing like being a walking and talking medical case study or an excellent subject for a doctor-in-training to publish a paper in a medical journal. I was told I was unique, special, and rare. Unlucky, but kind of lucky, because my villains were nonaggressive, slow-growing aliens who didn't choose to return to their planet.

They usually report extraterrestrials leaving the crime scene after abducting victims, but mine had infiltrated and were comfortable. These facts presented two realizations: (1) It was too late to build a border wall. (2) I couldn't time travel to capture future medical knowledge and return it to the present since there are no working DeLoreans on Craigslist.

I was scared, but alive and in otherwise decent health.

The unabridged diagnosis implied an ultimate form of irony. Living with a host of villains capable of attacking my nerves if they expanded their invasion was *unnerving*.

FOREVER SEEMS like a long time until you realize it could just mean one brief second or two after your last inhale, or maybe a few more if you're a deep-breathing enthusiast. That's how my father-in-law tricks the blood pressure test, an event more entertaining to watch than anything trending these days, and which might even prompt the most devout yogi to reconsider their training. The doctor informed me we would see each other *forever*, thanks to a rare condition that wouldn't ever be 100 percent curable. The definition of *forever* in this context was unequivocal: "Until one of us dies. Maybe you, or maybe me. Sorry."

That meant MRIs forever.

Follow-up appointments forever.

The incisive whisper resonating in the back of my mind that my concept of forever could end as unexpectedly as a violent sneeze, and I assure you it was not a soothing-wind-hitting-the-leaves kind of whisper. It was as unappealing as a sinister jab in the ribs and a villainous cackle by a heavy smoker with a grating accent that might haunt me forever when I'm mindlessly mowing the yard, collecting rotten pears, or ripping through 59 seconds of the "Minute Waltz."

The cloud of uncertainty attached to my diagnosis was horrible, and knowing what might very well kill me is some heavy shit to process. I assure you, no amount of conscious breathing can dissolve it, even though I'm always informed by every single medical visit that my blood pressure is fucking fantastic. At least I have that going for me because yoga sounds like a lot of work, I enjoy drinking beer too much, and dietary restrictions make as much sense as a food pyramid replaced by a plate. I don't really care, anyway, because by the time the government replaces the plate with a bowl, I'll probably be dead, and the UFOs will have torched Congress before anyone can save us all from "the grays."

A LIVING ROOM NEAR BOSTON

THE PHOTOGRAPHIC FLASHBACK

JULY 2021

POISON IVY IS A LUSH, harlotry character in comic books, the girl you don't bring home for your parents to meet. It is also more commonly recognized as an encroaching weed turning our property line and decomposing shed into an entangled jungle. Most people can be seen running down the aisle for calamine lotion when inadvertently plagued by the infamous three-leaved rash. However, since I'm rarer than a diamond in a copper mine, it should come as no surprise my superpower is a remarkable immunity to poison ivy. I can roll around in it all day if I want to, but I'm really not that motivated or daring.

THANKS to the convenience of "the cloud," I was quickly reminded of past exploits with historical imagery. In the tumultuous weeks following my surgery, somewhere around World UFO Day, Michelle and I were browsing our documented past because I couldn't do anything else except stare at the poison ivy taking over our backyard.

In our last photo together in Arizona, we were recently

married and visiting for a week. It was probably better than our first photograph together because technology had advanced significantly over 10 years, and a sneaky traffic speed camera hadn't blacked my face out. But, sometimes, the first or last of anything is not the most memorable, and the one selfie I always remember is at the top of a cloudy Mount Lemmon in November 2011. We were a month away from the fall semester ending, and I was about to graduate early due to realizing at the last minute that student loan funding is capped. I had reached that limit, was taking some extra classes, and planned on accepting an internship in DC, so the plan for independence and success wasn't extinguished yet.

Tucson was a sprawling mess of a city, even though it looked relatively small from the mountain peak scenic lookout. The view was much better than the anxiety-fueled and dismal feeling we shared. Future careers were only looking half promising, and mounting debt was suffocating, even at sea level. Most of the people I met in DC broke up with their significant others after college because careers seemed to take precedence over maintaining relationships. Love doesn't write the checks to FedLoan or pay the rent, but if there was one thing I wanted more than anything else, it was to stay with Michelle forever. That's what I remember thinking at the top of the mountain at 21, and I guess although most things have changed since then, that one thing has not.

HOSPITAL IN HOUSTON, TEXAS

A STRANGE SUMMER SIESTA

JULY 2021

I TRY NOT to be a selfish prick because sometimes being a regular prick is too much for Michelle to handle. Her arm was sore because it had been pricked by someone administering the COVID vaccine, affecting her mood. My arm wasn't sore because I didn't give a shit about vaccines and pandemics when more nefarious phenomena were trying to kill me. However, I felt a little tired from packing the backpack, performing its best impression of a suitcase, and post-surgery muscle tightness was still affecting my back.

I was doing my best not to complain.

WE HAD to hurry because the flight was booked last minute, and by the time we had found parking and gone through the TSA line, we would just make it if we didn't hit traffic, lace our shoes, and left the laptop at home. Or get in line behind one of those families with four children who were all the same age with miniature backpacks full of contraband that always turns out to be a few hundred feet of knotted-up electronics. An accident could really fuck things up, but I tried to suppress the possibility of a delay because the creaky stairs I was attempting to haul luggage down sometimes tripped me up, even though I should have been used to them by now. Reaching the last step seemed like an accomplishment and as satisfying as a middle finger to the translucent stair-tripping prick, so I sighed and felt a little better despite all my problems.

I was convinced someone was pranking me on the stairs every other week, and I'm now subscribing to the notion that it's a devious ghost who accumulates points for tripping people. But that's probably bullshit. There's no real reason to jump to unprovable conclusions: An old house isn't haunted just because it's old, creaky, crooked, and my life has spiraled out of control since we moved into it.

That must be pure coincidence, right? *Mister Cane can't be real.*

Just as I was throwing the bags into the back of our ride, something inside the house was wailing. The smoke detector.

Not again.

The invisible prick was setting it off for the past few weeks for no apparent reason.

Maybe we shouldn't have snapped the old cane.

There was only time to deactivate the device. I had no time to launch a paranormal investigation. We had to go straight to Logan to land in Texas to hear a second medical opinion. I wished I was going to Arizona instead or doing something belated for my birthday that was nearly canceled in 2021. Still, you can't have your cake and eat it too because sometimes desserts disappear in a haunted New England house if you leave something unattended for a few minutes. At least, that's what Michelle tells me. I don't really care if the house is some form of supernatural circus, Michelle is a sweet tooth con artist, nothing monumental happens for my birthday, or there isn't some fantastic "vacay" booked. I just don't want my life to be canceled for a very long time. That would be as nice as not being tripped on the stairs by cats or ghosts or having Cheerios thrown at you by a gang of screaming children on a very long nonstop flight to Houston.

SECOND OPINIONS ARE SOMETIMES as delectable as leftover pizza that sat on the counter overnight because someone forgot to put it in the fridge or the hotel room didn't have one. If you're starving the next day, you may eat a questionable slice, but it might make you beeline for the bottle of Tums. Although Houston primarily draws space enthusiasts and Star Trek nerds, I was only interested in its world-renowned medical facilities and their contribution to ependymoma research. We verified the Tex-Mex was good and tried the pizza, but I've had better slices in Phoenix or Philadelphia and realized I also had more appealing *first* medical opinions in Boston.

Our arrival was greeted by homeless panhandlers who held handwritten signs illegibly drawn on used pizza boxes, requesting financial donations. The contrast couldn't have been more different from the gold-lined streets back East and as glamorous as getting a shot of "contrast" to round out a two-hour MRI. Unsurprisingly, Michelle was unused to these solicitations since Boston is as wealthy as cold.

I locked the car door any time we rolled to a stop, wondering if my problems were better or worse than those of the homeless. The subsequent medical consultations were as reassuring as envisioning the homeless people's future, confirming the unfortunate nature of the disease by yet another world-class medical team. The attitude differed from Boston; a sense of profound urgency conflicted with the doctors I was assigned, giving Michelle and I an uneasy weight to carry around on the visit. The underlying tone seemed a direct contradiction to what we were used to, mystifying the specialists we met, who seemed to insinuate something like, *"What, are they stoned and asleep up there in Beantown, waiting for the alien tumors to win? It's time to go to war, son."*

I didn't know we were going to war until we landed in Texas, getting the feeling there was no time for sabbaticals or coffee breaks—this *was a serious matter.* We left the medical complex more anxious than when we arrived, wondering if our current approach was too passive. The doctor with an unplaceable accent scared me more than the pizza hobos, giving me an institutional, procedural lecture and a repeated shake of the head, suggesting *yes, I was indeed too complacent and possibly screwed. You probably need lots of radiation, buddy. Deal with it.*

I wish we had taken a real vacation like everyone else in the airport probably was doing instead of getting some thorough reassurances that more tumor boards would review my file, suggesting I need to nuke my brain and everything else because, hell, they don't mess around in Texas. Their studies showed radiation could eradicate my specific aliens, unless they returned. Which happened about *50 percent* of the time.

I barely passed business statistics, but the verdict sounded as confident as a coin toss, and I'm not a victim of the Monte Carlo fallacy.

Huh, if my return flight had a 50 percent chance of success, I think I'd rather drive back in the rental, even invite a hobo or two. Perhaps the chance of them murdering me is about 50 percent?

THE ADVENTURE in Houston marked the six-week sabbatical since my surgery. It was a welcome, albeit stressful, break from all the chaos consuming our lives and from getting repeatedly beat up at work while my nerves were being attacked by aliens. As most of my coworkers believe, I had back surgery because I didn't know how to "lift correctly." Everyone's experienced that before, so it's usually everyone's first assumption, and since everyone's already used to accepting fake news as fact, I just agree. And probably because good ole' Doctor Summeroff was generous in his recommendation for extended sick leave. What luck!

Yeah, I'm a lucky guy. I had a good doctor's note and paid off someone in the union and suddenly was lazy for the first time in my life. I wanted to sit on my ass dreaming of Arizona instead of showing up to work. Now everyone will probably run to their doctors and ask for time off because the "young kid who looks healthy somehow had the entire summer off." Life isn't fair. I guess I'll let them think that because remaining reticent while everyone with no real problems gets pissed and jealous feels better than when the words *tumor, neurosurgeon, lumbar drain, laminectomy, radiation,* or *oncology* leave my mouth, so I avoid saying them. Now I know why white lies exist and why some people work from home. Office culture can be more grating than the block of Romano that Michelle's Italian family breaks out for every meal, and I guess I'll have to pass on both.

Sorry, ancestry enthusiasts, I might be more German than Italian, but probably just as French and somehow 100 percent lactose intolerant.

THE TRIP back home was bumpy and crowded, and the filtered oxygen on the plane was stuffy. This time the airline sandwiched my pale green wife in a middle seat, stuck next to a man-bun kid eating a sandwich from a vintage pale green Tupperware container. It was difficult to relax. I was on edge, contemplating what Boston would recommend after the upcoming MRI scheduled for the following day and how different that would be from the Texans' suggestion to wage nuclear war on the overrun border.

The airport in Houston is named after former president Bush. It seemed like the decision to hit my enemies with everything in the arsenal was indeed a Texan doctrine extending beyond foreign policy. This is probably comforting and acceptable for some people, but I had my reservations.

I just don't want to become a civilian casualty left on the side of the road with a head reduced to a bowl of pudding, holding up a greasy sign asking for charity because the world isn't fair. Besides, carpet bombing often displaces the innocent and still doesn't stop Al-Qaeda.

If that was my fate, I knew exactly where I'd claim my curb, waving at all the expensive German cars driven by Starbucks-addicted doctors with my cardboard pizza box sign. I knew whom I'd haunt every day with darting, hollow eyes and a paranoid parade at traffic stoplights.

While eating pathetic miniature pretzels almost too small to pick up and a Dutch wafer too sticky to let go, I couldn't help but analyze my past and figure out why my life's story took such a tragic and unanticipated turn. It was more unexpected than the wild recklessness of Houston drivers who couldn't judge curbs and other traffic. My mind drifted to a cactus-lined utopia where the glaring sun killed all the pessimistic notions of radiation-induced trauma. The absence of humidity made breathing effortless in the desert, and the crystal clear sky seemed to comfort any restless soul.

I SNAPPED back to reality when a passenger across the aisle spilled his soda and ice, and it splashed onto my leg. *Huh, my pandemic face mask didn't save me from that fate.*

"Sorry, bro."

"Yeah, no problem," I lied. I would have known where this plane was headed, even if no one had told me.

I stared at the ice cube in the aisle, forming a puddle, *just like the sidewalk puddles that would probably ruin my future pizza box sign when a six-figure SUV with a vanity plate rolled past, oblivious to my misfortune.*

The adversity experienced over the past two months felt like a sniper had me in his sights. Even though I dodged a bullet at the last second, there were several rounds left in the chamber, ready to take me out when I least expected it. Perhaps I should live life like a reckless gambler, flipping coins and deciding my actions based on chance? If I knew my future would be a losing battle with shifty prick alien fuckers or the repercussions of nuclear fallout exposure, I should've lived more dangerously. *Fuck the employee 401(k) match, emergency fund, checking account "buffer," and Roths.* I should've gone hot-air ballooning or skydiving, invested in cryptocurrency, joined special forces, or taken a *John Wick*-style martial arts class to prepare for a job delivering pizza in a city like Houston.

I tried to fall asleep on the plane, tired of thinking about Texas and had run out of distracting books to read. The airlines had stopped serving alcohol because of COVID, and the in-flight internet was out, so there was nothing else to do. The nap was fitful, and when I groggily woke up to the seat belt chimes and a garbled pilot greeting about temperatures and altitude, I rechecked my pocket for a fateful $50 bill.

Nope, not yet. I'm not dead yet.

Even if most of my dreams are bad, good music doesn't get adequate airtime, and my snakebite reality is some Poe/Lovecraft mash-up with a 21st-century technological twist, at least I can dream again. That's a welcome change from nerve pain and no sleep. After all, I'm no sleepless bullfrog or elephant, but damn, I could go for some tacos and a desert tailgate party in a particular Ranger with Michelle. Head up to the Enchanted Forest afterward, somewhere beyond Lynx Lake, and admire where the pines grow.

That's a narrative I like a lot better than whoever's penning the script of my dreams.

THE RECURRING dream for me is never a comforting one. It's always a borderline nightmare, where assassins break into my home and steal my car for some unknown reason. If they knew how unlucky all my vehicles were, maybe they would have gone after someone else's, but I'm always helpless in the dream and frustratingly unsuccessful at conveying my concerns.

Lock the doors—you know they're going to show up, somehow.

I don't know if they send a warning or something or announce it on a megaphone.

Load the gun, but it never shoots—must be bad ammo.

The assassin-dream villains are always trying to break in, and they seem to always do despite locked or barricaded doors, and of course, I run from them like Forrest Gump because it looks like that's the only action I'm good at in the dreamworld. Much to my frustration, the dream always plays out like the Alamo, and at some point when I'm losing and asking John Wayne for a cigarette, I wake up. But it's nice now to dream of the villains because when I wake up, I realize dreaming means I've been asleep for a solid eight hours. I'll take that over a groggy and cringeworthy intermission to perpetual pseudoscience programming any day or night.

FINALE

IT'S hard to believe that just over a decade ago, I was gunning and hiking through the Southwest, brimming with optimism. Now I'm stalled out in the Northeast, in shock, letting 10-year outlooks sink in and staring at a business card for Dana-Farber tacked onto my groaning fridge. I'm also staring out the old warbly window of a haunted historical home, admiring the rescued cedar tree I finally planted in the ground in August, by myself, with a shovel, with no villains holding me back.

About fucking time.

I think it may actually have a chance. It's closer to green again.

Trying to comprehend what's happening is as unbelievable as one of those sad *60 Minutes* episodes they follow up with a year later to inform us who is still alive, and *you* are the person they mention in the credits the second you are thinking "couldn't happen to me." My outlook seems promising, although uncertain, as my post-surgery nerve pain has magically melted away quicker than a springtime Arizona snowstorm. I haven't taken a single pain pill either and plan on donating lots of cherry juice to the Red Cross or our local food pantry— whoever needs it more. If my past showed my future, I would unquestionably be screwed. But now that my true enemy has been exposed, and as my screwed-together back is mainly healed, I remain optimistic and convinced sometimes you should embrace extended contracts, automatic transmissions, and comfortable suspensions.

Listening to what your body is telling you could save years of pain and misdiagnosed villains from wreaking havoc on your existence, especially when the signs are subtle at first before slowly hijacking and eventually derailing a once-normal life. I was warned, and now I'm fully aware of their capabilities and intentions, and dammit, I will fight those alien bastards until one of us wins. I hope it's me.

IN THE MEANTIME, I may return to Arizona with my wife and a newer uncursed Lincoln, ignore student loans, houses, financial planning, all the life "achievement milestones" documented daily by insecure people, *and just live*. Perhaps those Sedona hippies living among the red healing energy rocks are onto something. Or, maybe, I'll go join the real Nitro Circus, sell postal trade secrets, or write a book about all these potential adventures while I sip a bold dark roast from the comfort of a camper trailer overlooking a desert oasis where villains will never find me. Maybe somewhere between Bumble Bee and Cottonwood.

That would be nice.

After all, *what else am I supposed to do*?

The Cursed Lincoln

ABOUT THE AUTHOR

A. H. Nazzareno is busy writing and just happy to be alive.